YOU CAN RUN
BUT
YOU CAN'T HIDE

YOU CAN RUN
but
YOU CAN'T HIDE

Grange
BOOKS

First published in 2000 as
Stumped on a Sticky Wicket

Reprinted for Grange Books in 2003

an imprint of Grange Books PLC
The Grange
Kingsnorth Industrial Estate
Hoo nr Rochester
Kent
UK
ME3 9ND
www.grangebooks.co.uk

Typeset by David Onyett, Publishing & Production Services,
Cheltenham
Printed in Thailand for Imago Publishing

Introduction

Organized sports and games, in the sense that they are played and watched today, are comparatively recent developments. Football (soccer), to take perhaps the most popular sport today, developed from a game played in the Middle Ages, but this was little more than a free-for-all in which any number of participants pursued a ball for several hours in a mêlée unfettered by rules or time limits.

It is only in the last century and a half that a significant proportion of the population have had enough free time to allow them to play or watch sports and games. Until then, 'leisure activities' enjoyed by tens of millions today were only available to the majority of people on a few religious feast days. For the rest of the year life revolved around the daily need to provide shelter and sustenance.

Of course there were some activities, regarded as sports these days, which played an important part in national life in the Middle Ages. Archery is an obvious example. From the reign of Henry I to that of Elizabeth I, regular archery practice was compulsory for all able-bodied men, and this became a feature of weekly life in towns and villages throughout the country, where practice at the butts took place after Sunday morning worship. The value and success of such a policy was proved on many medieval battlefields in which troops of well-trained British archers, armed with the longbow, devastated opposing forces with the speed and accuracy of their firepower.

However, until the middle of the nineteenth century, only the well-to-do had the time and resources to devote to the range of sports and games as we know them today. So it is inevitable that their pastimes should be among the earliest 'sporting' and 'gaming' contributions to the English language.

Hunting, in its many forms, cockfighting, horse racing, prize-fighting and gambling (at cards or dice) have provided English with a broad mix of terms and phrases that have been taken up in general usage. When we speak of 'beating about the bush', 'skirting round' an issue or being 'in at the kill' few of us give any thought to the hunting field where these metaphors evolved. The same is no doubt true of metaphors from dice games, such as 'a brace of shakes' and 'at sixes and sevens'. Card games too have supplied general terms like 'underhand', 'ace' and 'across the board', as well as the range of specific terms from whist, bridge, poker and other games, that have subsequently acquired a place in everyday speech.

Athletics ranks as one of the oldest organized sporting activities, with a recorded history which dates back to the Olympic Games of ancient Greece. In cases like this, the changing nature and development of the sport can be seen in the variance of terms like 'starting from scratch' (which described the traditional way of marking a starting-line in the dirt) and 'breasting the tape', (which conjures images of modern athletics races that end with 'photo-finishes' and 'split-second' results).

The growing popularity and influence of sports and games is also reflected in the recent application of specific sporting terminology to other aspects of life and work. 'Spin doctors', 'rain checks' and 'league tables', all of which are fairly recent arrivals in everyday speech, owe their current usage to the popularity of baseball and football in which they were first coined.

The sporting heritage of hundreds of everyday words and phrases, revealed in the pages that follow, confirms the diversity of sports and games that have been developed and shaped in the English-speaking world throughout the history of the English language.

Above board

Dr Johnson was in no doubt about the meaning and origin of 'above board'. As the great dictionary compiler explained, to be 'above board' is to be honest and open; the expression is one 'borrowed from gamesters, who, when they put their hands under the table, are changing their cards.' This amounts to cheating, of course. Anyone changing their cards is acting in an 'underhand' way by illicitly improving their chances of winning. When all play is 'above board', there can be no suspicion of trickery and the same applies when the phrase is used in any other context.

According to Hoyle

Edmond Hoyle was an authority on card games who lived from 1672 until 1769. He was nicknamed the 'Father of Whist' following the success of his book *A Short Treatise on the Game of Whist* which was published in 1742. This regulated the rules of the game and remained the standard work until 1864, when the rules were changed. Six years after the appearance of his book on whist, Hoyle added handbooks on backgammon, brag, chess, piquet and quadrille. Together these formed a definitive work, *Hoyle's Standard Games*, and the weight of their authority gave rise to the idiom 'according to Hoyle', meaning 'according to the best usage' and 'on the best authority'.

Ace

In ancient Rome and throughout the Roman Empire an *as* was a unit of weight, equating to a 'pound'. In time, *as* acquired the associated meaning of 'unity' and a 'unit'. The word passed unchanged into Old French and then modern French. In English *as* became 'ace' and by the thirteenth century it had come to signify a throw of 'one' at dice. A century later 'ace' was being used for a playing card bearing one pip (reckoned to be of the highest value). Robert Burns, writing in the second half of the eighteenth century, used 'ace' in the sense of the 'highest' or the 'best'. During the First World War the French *as* was applied to a pilot who shot down ten or more enemy aircraft. This meaning was soon adopted by its English counterpart and, from describing an expert flier, 'ace' became a hallmark of excellence achieved by the 'best' in a wide range of human activities, notably those involving sport or other physical endeavours.

Ace in the hole

This is an expression, coined in America, which equates to 'having an ace up your sleeve'. The term derives from stud poker where an 'ace in the hole' is a 'hidden advantage'. The 'hole' card is one which remains hidden until the betting has been completed. If it happens to be an ace, that's all to the good for the player holding it.

Aerial Ping-Pong

'Aerial Ping-Pong' is a tongue-in-cheek nickname for Australian Rules football, in which players are allowed to kick and punch the ball, but may not throw it. This results in a style of play involving a considerable amount of jumping, kicking and catching as play moves from one team to the other.

Against the clock

In this expression speed is of the essence and anything undertaken 'against the clock' has to be finished by a set time. The allusion is to a race that is timed by a stopwatch or similar device. Races 'against the clock' often form a part of training, allowing competitors to participate under racing conditions to improve on previous performances, or to measure themselves against the times set by likely opponents.

All at sixes and sevens

When a situation is 'all at sixes and sevens' it is in a state of confusion and disorder. The allusion, in a gaming context, is to a game of dice.

Also-ran

In horse racing an 'also-ran' refers to a horse which fails to finish among the first three runners. Classified as an 'also-ran', the horse is lumped together with 'the rest of the field'. The phrase is now applied away from the racecourse to anyone who fails to make a mark or distinguish themselves.

Anchorman

'Anchor' is a very old word, appearing in present-day English almost unchanged from its Latin antecedent *ancora*. As the name suggests, an 'anchorman' is a key member of a team, coming at the end of a line (like a metaphorical anchor) and acting as the last, and most important, part of that line. 'Anchormen' are found in two events on the athletics field: the tug of war and the relay race. In the tug of war, the anchorman is the end man, who secures the rope by passing it over one shoulder and under the opposite arm. In a relay race the 'anchor man' is the last member of a team, the one who runs the final leg of the race to the finish line. From athletics, the expression has passed into other areas of life. Television news broadcasts now refer to presenters who co-ordinate news bulletins and interviews as 'anchormen', and 'anchormen' act as key figures in commerce and other sporting arenas as well.

Ashes series

Since 1882 cricket test matches between England and Australia have been contested for the mythical prize known as the 'Ashes'. The term arose from a newspaper article printed after Australia defeated England at the Oval in 1882. This was the first time that they had beaten England in England and on 29 August that year the *Sporting Times* printed a mock obituary to English cricket, which ended 'the body will be cremated and the Ashes taken to Australia'. The following year England gained their revenge and beat Australia in Australia. Their victory inspired two Melbourne ladies to present the England Captain, the Hon. Ivo Bligh, with an urn containing the ashes of the stumps and bails. This has remained in the pavilion at Lord's since it was brought home by Bligh's victorious touring side. When either country 'wins the Ashes', it retains them until beaten, although the urn itself never leaves its London home.

At bay

To be 'at bay' is to be in a position of defence when cornered by pursuers. The expression has a long history, originating in the language of the medieval hunt. 'Bay' in this usage refers to the 'baying' of hounds, barking after cornering their prey. This hunted animal is therefore 'at bay' when, driven to desperation, it faces its barking pursuers.

At fault

This is such a commonly used expression that its origin is seldom given a second thought. We speak of individuals being 'at fault' if they are in the wrong, or have committed a misdemeanour. However, 'at fault' originated as a specific term in the hunting field. It referred to a pack of hounds who had lost the scent they should have been following and were either following the wrong one, or were milling around following no scent at all.

Backing the wrong horse

'Backing' has a number of meanings in English, but when 'back' is used as a verb it generally has the sense of 'supporting' in some way. This is the case in this instance. 'Backing' a horse, meaning 'to place a bet on it', amounts to an abbreviation for 'backing your opinion' that the horse will finish the race in a particular position. In doing this, you 'support' your judgement and the conclusion you have reached by wagering a sum of money on the outcome of the race. If your judgement proves faulty and the horse fails to finish in the predicted position, you evidently 'backed the wrong horse'. From its racing application, 'backing the wrong horse' has acquired the broader meaning for 'making an error of judgement' in general.

Back to square one

'Back to square one' originated from a game of some sort; the question is which game precisely. There are two principal contenders: football and Snakes and Ladders. The argument in favour of football dates from the early days of radio commentaries of football matches given by the BBC. To help listeners follow the passage of play, the *Radio Times* printed a map of the football pitch divided into numbered squares, which commentators called out as play moved from square to square. When the ball went into 'square one', the argument runs that the commentary went 'back to square one'. The weakness in this line of thought is that there is no reason why 'square one' should have been the 'starting point'. After a stoppage play could have recommenced from any square on the pitch, which might or might not have been 'square one'. The 'Snakes and Ladders' theory does offer a logical return to 'square one', or close to it. Any player unlucky enough to land on one of the long snakes running from near the top of the board, risks sliding back down almost to the very beginning, or 'back to square one'.

Backing the field

This is another turn of phrase connected with placing bets on horse races. To 'back the field' means to bet on all the horses in a race except one, the favourite.

Ball in your court

If you are told that the 'ball is in your court', the meaning is the same as 'it's your turn now'. The 'court' in question is one player's part of the tennis court; not the lawn tennis court familiar today, but its predecessor where 'real tennis' or 'royal tennis' has been played since the Middle Ages. This is a game similar in many ways to lawn tennis, but now played on a smooth surface in a 'court' surrounded by walls and sloping roofs which form part of the playing area. Only a small number of real tennis courts remain in use today, but it was a popular medieval pastime, notably among lower orders of the clergy. Originally the game existed in two forms: *longue paume*, which was played in unenclosed, open spaces, and *courte paume*, the enclosed version that is still played. Until the beginning of the sixteenth century *le jeu de paume*, to give 'real tennis' its French name, was played by hitting a ball with the palm of the hand, in a similar way to playing fives. The long-handled racket strung with sheep's intestines was not introduced until 1500, or thereabouts. Over the following century France went 'real tennis' mad. By 1600 there were over 1,000 'courts' of various designs in Paris alone; about a quarter of these were enclosed courts. The game was well known in England as well. Shakespeare makes a string of references to it in *Henry V*, in the scene in which the Dauphin of France seeks to slight the young King of England by sending him a gift of tennis balls in answer to his hereditary claim to a number of dukedoms in France. This is part of King Henry's reply:

When we have matched our rackets to these balls,
We will in France, by God's grace, play a set
Shall strike his father's crown into the hazard.
Tell him he hath made a match with such a wrangler
That all the courts of France will be disturbed
With chases.

Ballpark

In America a 'ballpark' is a large stadium in which baseball is played. During the second half of the twentieth century 'ballpark' became widely used in the sense of a very rough 'estimate' (sometimes referred to as a 'guesstimate'). The expression is often applied to financial dealings, hence the phrase 'ballpark figure'. When it was first coined, the expression frequently took the form of 'in the same ballpark', meaning that the sums being discussed were of reasonably similar size.

Ball tampering

In cricket, 'ball tampering' is the illegal process of changing the surface of the ball to affect its movement in the air. This can be achieved by fingering the seam, or even cutting the stitches in extreme cases, as well as by rubbing one side of the ball with abrasive materials, such as sand or dirt, all of which accentuate the natural flight of the ball. 'Ball tampering' favours a bowling side and in the early 1990s allegations that it had been used by some international test cricket teams fuelled considerable controversy in the game worldwide.

Bandy

'Bandy' is a game, first developed in Ireland, which is played like a primitive form of hockey. Players are divided into two teams and each player is equipped with a stick with a crook at the end. The ball is 'bandied' between them as each team tries to drive it into the opposing team's goal. A modern form of bandy is played on ice. This shares many similarities with ice hockey, although it is played on a larger rink, no play is allowed behind the goals and the players strike a ball rather than a puck. The origin of the name 'bandy' may be connected with 'real tennis' (above). There are references from the early seventeenth century to 'bandying at tennis' and the modern use of 'bandy' in the sense of 'wrangle' alludes to the knocking to and fro of a ball both in tennis and the early form of hockey.

Barking up the wrong tree

To be 'barking up the wrong tree' implies that you are wasting your efforts or directing them in the wrong direction. It could also be said that you are 'following the wrong scent', which comes close to the origin of the phrase that is derived from a method of hunting racoons in North America. This takes place in the dark and uses dogs to mark the trees up which the racoons escape. However, it is not uncommon for the dogs to be mistaken and, when this happens, their owners find them 'barking up the wrong tree' while the racoon has slipped away to safety in another part of the woodland.

Barracking

Jeering and ironic cheering has been known as 'barracking' since the nineteenth century. It is a feature of sporting events attended by large crowds of opposing supporters, and of political meetings and Parliamentary debates. 'Barracking' acquired its unusual name in Australia towards the end of the nineteenth century where it was applied to the noisy response of crowds, watching cricket or football matches, who took an exception to something on the field of play. One explanation suggests that 'barracking' came into being as a blend of the aboriginal word *borak*, which means 'fun' or 'chaffing', and the Cockney 'barrakin' meaning a 'jumble of words'. An alternative explanation draws on the Victoria Barracks in Melbourne, which was close to a field where football games were played. These attracted large unruly crowds of spectators who became known as 'barrackers'.

Battle royal

Until it was made illegal in 1849, cockfighting had been a popular pastime in England since the twelfth century. Henry VIII added a 'cockpit' at Whitehall Palace and in the following century James I and Charles II were enthusiastic followers of what later came to be seen as a cruel blood sport. 'Battle royal' was a term in cockfighting for a particular type of contest in which a number of birds were placed in the cockpit to fight against each other until there was only one survivor; that bird became the victor of the 'battle royal'. From the mayhem and confusion that would have erupted in the early stages of such a contest, the expression 'battle royal' acquired its metaphorical sense of a 'mêlée' or 'contest of wits'.

Beating about the bush

In the sporting field, game of all sorts take refuge in thickets. Huntsmen, whether using dogs, nets or shotguns, always approach with caution areas of undergrowth or dense woodland where game might be hiding. Teams of 'beaters' frequently surround the 'bush' and then move through it systematically, driving the game towards the hunters. From this the term 'beating about the bush' has been applied to approaching a subject cautiously and in a roundabout way, rather than tackling it head-on.

Beat to the punch

Boxing, like cockfighting, is another long-established sport. Though far more strictly regulated than it was in the past, boxing has survived as a sporting contest between two equally matched opponents, unlike cockfighting and similar blood sports. To 'beat [an opponent] to the punch' is a term from the boxing ring describing the speed and agility of a boxer who is able to hit an opponent before his punch, launched first, can land. Away from the boxing ring, 'beating to the punch' is used metaphorically of any 'fast-workers' who are 'quick on their feet' and capable of acting forcefully and resolutely without delay.

Behind the eight ball

This is an expression from snooker or pool, in which the 'eight ball' should be the last left on the table. To be 'behind the eight ball' places you in an awkward predicament, which is the metaphorical meaning of the phrase.

Below the belt

Boxing underwent significant changes following the adoption of a set of regulations drawn up in 1867 under the patronage of the Marquess of Queensberry, after whom they were named. These formed the basis of modern glove-fighting as opposed to earlier 'bare-knuckle' contests and within thirty years they had been adopted for world professional championship matches. Among their regulations, the Queensberry Rules banned the hitting of an opponent below the waistband, or 'belt'. Within a short time, hitting 'below the belt' became a widely-used expression for behaving in an 'unsporting' and possibly 'cowardly' way.

Bingo

Games in which players marked numbered cards according to numbers drawn at random and called aloud had been popular long before the name 'Bingo' was coined. 'Lotto', 'Keno', 'Loo' and 'Housey-Housey' all followed the same principle, but 'Bingo' superseded these during the growth of its popularity in the twentieth century. Edwin Lowe is credited with starting the craze, following his visit to a carnival in Florida where he was inspired by watching people playing what they called 'bean-o', a game in which their cards were marked by beans placed over the numbers called. Apparently one of Lowe's friends stammered 'B . . . b . . . bingo' in his excitement at winning and so gave 'Bingo' its distinctive name. The word already existed in English as the name for a form of brandy, but this was quickly eclipsed as the popularity for Lowe's new game of chance swept through America and then overseas; in the course of which 'Bingo' acquired its additional meaning as an exclamation of success.

Blazer

In 1845 the captain of HMS *Blazer* decided to dress his boat's crew in blue and white striped jerseys. This soon led to the jerseys being nicknamed 'Blazers'. The style of wearing similarly brightly striped jackets was adopted by sporting clubs that were being established at this time. Rowing crews in particular popularized 'blazers' which carried the colours of their respective boat clubs. In time 'blazers' were divided into two categories: brightly coloured sporting ones and the more sober, dark-coloured ones, that became a part of many school uniforms.

Bluff

'Bluffing' in any context implies 'deceiving by pretence' and 'calling' someone's 'bluff' means revealing such a deception. 'Bluffing' is an accepted ruse in several card games, whereby a player bets heavily on a weak hand, in the hope that an opponent will throw in his cards and forfeit his stake rather than chance them against what is imagined to be a superior hand. 'Bluff', in this context, was first used in America where it may well have been coined from the Dutch *bluffen*, meaning to 'brag' or 'boast'.

Board of green cloth

In the last century the 'board of green cloth' has become slang for a card-table or billiard-table. Until the end of the eighteenth century, however, the Board of Green Cloth was an official body holding an important position in the English royal household. Seated at a green-covered table, the committee under the chairmanship of the Lord Steward scrutinized the accounts of the royal household and also handled all offences that occurred within the bounds of the palace. In 1782 the Board of Green Cloth lost its executive powers and its duties were restricted to royal domestic arrangements, with the Master of the Household appointed at its head.

Body blow

Receiving a 'body blow' means to receive a severe setback which 'knocks the wind' out of you. The expression comes from the boxing ring where a 'body blow' is the term used for a punch landed between the breast-bone and the navel. Struck here with force, it can have the effect of stopping an opponent abruptly by winding him.

Bossing your shot

Archery may not be as widely practised as it once was, but a sport with such a long history inevitably leaves its mark on the language. In archery, a 'boss' is the straw-filled base to which a target is attached. Those unfortunate enough to miss the target completely and fire their arrows into the 'boss' were mocked by more accurate archers who would call them 'boss-eyed'. From this early reference 'bossing your shot' has developed the meaning of missing your shot completely. As archery declined, 'boss-eyed' developed an auxiliary meaning in slang as a reference to an injured or defective eye.

Breadbasket

In boxing, 'breadbasket' is a euphemism for the 'stomach'.

Breaking your duck

Cricket is another game which has provided English with a number of enduring expressions, of which 'breaking your duck' is one. Players going in to bat start their innings with a score of nought. If they are dismissed before scoring any runs, they are 'out for a duck' (the origin of 'duck' is discussed below). However, scoring their first runs 'breaks their duck' and, from the cricket pitch, 'breaking your duck' has been put to use in any number of situations in which an individual starts to make progress by achieving the first recognized goal or objective.

Breasting the tape

The allusion here is to athletics and track races in which competitors race over various distances. These all end at the finish line, marked by a tape positioned at chest height. The athlete who breaks the tape with his or her torso is the winner and 'breasting the tape' means succeeding by finishing something just ahead of the 'rest of the field'.

Bridge

In less than two hundred years 'bridge' has become one of the world's most popular card games. Developed from the older game of whist, 'bridge' was first played in Turkey and the Near East in the second half of the nineteenth century. Its Levantine origin may help to explain the derivation of the name 'bridge', which appears to have come from a Russian version of the game called *biritch*.

By a long chalk

It was once customary for many games to be scored by making chalk marks on a slate or other convenient surface. A long line of chalk marks indicated a clear winner and 'by a long chalk' acquired the meaning 'thoroughly', as in an expression like 'He beat me by a long chalk'. The phrase is used almost as much in a negative context, in which 'not by a long chalk' is an equally emphatic statement that something or someone will fail in a particular undertaking.

Caddie

A 'caddie' today is found almost exclusively on a golf-course, either as an assistant who carries a player's clubs and offers assistance within the rules of the game, or in the now more familiar form of a small cart in which a player either pushes his clubs or in which he rides with them. 'Caddie', like golf itself, is Scottish in origin. In its earliest form it was spelt 'caudie' and was used to describe an errand boy or porter. This meaning probably stemmed from the French *cadet*, the term used for a younger brother and later an attendant.

Calling off all bets

The literal meaning of 'calling off all bets' is to cancel all wagers in certain situations. This might happen if there is suspicion that a race or some other sporting event has been rigged to cheat bookmakers. In its wider meaning, 'calling off all bets' refers to 'repudiating a complicated or disadvantageous agreement or problem'.

Capped

Players who represent England, Scotland, Ireland or Wales in any of the major field sports is entitled to wear a cap bearing the national emblem. This has given rise to expressions like 'winning a first cap', which means making a first appearance in an international sporting contest.

Carry weight

To 'carry weight' is to have influence. An argument which 'carries weight' is substantial and forceful in the context in which it is put forward. In the same way, an individual 'carries weight' if his or her reputation or experience is recognized by others as being significant and influential. The term comes from horse racing, where weight carried by individual mounts is equalized by weight being added to the lighter ones.

Carrying all before

This is an expression of triumph and success. Anyone who 'carries all before them', wins all the prizes and figuratively carries them away from other competitors.

Carrying your bat

A player who opens an innings in cricket and who plays right through to the end without being dismissed is said to 'carry his [or her] bat'. The phrase is sometimes used in other situations with reference to people who last longer at something than anyone else.

Cashing in your chips

'Chips' in this expression are the counters used as tokens in gambling games. When players finish a session of playing such games, they return their chips to the casino and receive the equivalent sum in cash, hence 'cashing in your chips'. The expression is applied in slang as a euphemism for 'death', implying that those who have died no longer need their 'chips', which presumably allude to life itself.

Catch a crab

Rowing is the sport from which 'catching a crab' is derived. The phrase describes the plight of a rower who fails to remove his or her blade from the water at the end of a stroke. This usually happens because the blade has dug too deep into the water, or because it has been turned underwater and is therefore difficult to raise above the surface. The result is the same in either case: the momentum of the boat drives the handle of the blade into the rower's body, sometimes with such force that he or she is lifted from the seat and thrown overboard.

Caught out

'Catching' the ball after it has hit the hand or cricket bat of a player and before it touches the ground is one of the ways of dismissing players in cricket; players who lose their wickets in this way are described as having been 'caught out'. Other people, quite unconnected with cricket, can also be 'caught out' if they have been practising some sort of deception and are then revealed to have been lying or otherwise disguising the truth.

Cauliflower ear

Boxers whose ears suffer repeated injuries from being pummelled in boxing matches may develop 'cauliflower ears'. The condition is not restricted to boxing, though. Rugby is another sport in which this type of injury can occur. Taking its name from the shape of the surface of a cauliflower, a 'cauliflower ear' is permanently thickened and deformed by repeated swellings and damage to the tissue of the outer ear.

Charley Paddock

Charley Paddock was one of the world's greatest athletes in the first half of the twentieth century. A sprinter of exceptional versatility, he was known unofficially as the 'world's fastest man' for much of his track career. Between 1921 and 1926 he equalled the world record for the 100 yards six times and in 1921 set an unofficial record for the 100 metres which was not bettered until 1950. His speed and fame gave rise to the expression 'doing a Charley Paddock', which meant 'making your escape' by running away, notably from the police.

Checkmate

This is the call in a game of chess given at the move when your opponent's king is placed in an inextricable position of check. 'Checkmate' has been recorded in English since the fourteenth century and is derived, like the game itself, from the languages of the Middle East. In Persian *shah mat* means 'the king is helpless'.

Chipping in

'Chipping in' has two meanings: 'to interrupt' and 'to make a contribution', in the sense of 'Everyone chipped in to buy him a leaving present'. The latter is drawn from the game of poker, in which 'chips', representing money, are placed in the 'pot' by all the players.

Clean bowled

In cricket, a player who is batting is said to have been 'bowled' if the ball delivered by the bowler breaks his or her wicket. Players are said to be 'clean bowled' if their wickets are broken without the ball touching their bats or anything they are wearing. The phrase is sometimes used figuratively in circumstances when someone is comprehensively outwitted or metaphorically 'dismissed'.

Close of play

Many first-class cricket matches last longer than a single day and 'close of play' is the term for the end of play on a particular day of the match. As a general turn of phrase, 'close of play' is used in a similar way to mean 'the end of the working day' and the 'time when business stops for the day'; both of which convey the meaning that activities have been 'suspended for the day' but will be continued the following morning.

Come to blows

A 'blow' in boxing is a legitimate hit with the fist and when boxers 'come to blows' they close on each other to exchange punches. 'Coming to blows' is now widely used as a metaphor meaning 'to begin fighting'.

Coming up to scratch

'Coming up to scratch' is a term from both athletics and boxing. Until the comparatively recent introduction of starting blocks and running tracks with special surfaces, competitors for a running race used to line up along a line scratched in the ground. A similar line was used in early boxing matches as well, when both contestants had to begin each round standing with one foot touching a line scratched on the ground. If either of them failed 'to come up scratch' at the start of a round, he lost the fight. Since those times, 'coming up to scratch' has been used in the sense of 'achieving a recognized standard'. Failing to 'come up to scratch' means failing to live up to expectations.

Counted out

This is another phrase that started out in the boxing ring. If, during the course of a round, a boxer falls in the ring so that any part of his body other than his feet is touching the ground, he has ten seconds in which to stand up again. The referee calls the seconds so that the boxer knows how much longer he has to get to his feet; if he is still 'down' on the count of ten he loses the fight. To be 'counted out', then, means to be unable to get up before the count reaches ten. The phrase has become popular in general expressions like 'count me out' which means 'don't include me'.

Crew cut

Although short-cropped hair is a feature of the American army, it seems that the name 'crew cut' correctly reflects its origin. In the 1940s university oarsmen at Harvard and Yale took to wearing their hair cropped very short back and sides with a short, brushlike top. The style was adopted by athletes in other sports, but the oarsmen, or 'crew', established themselves as the trend-setters.

Cricket

Cricket, or games very like it, were played in several countries in the Middle Ages, but it was in England that cricket first became established and where it developed into the modern game. There is a reference to cricket being played in Kent, in the wardrobe accounts of Edward I for 1300. From the year 1550, there is a record of a coroner testifying that, as schoolboys in Guildford, he and his schoolmates went to a piece of ground in the parish of Holy Trinity 'and did runne and play there at creckett'. However, it was in the eighteenth century that cricket began to resemble the game played today. The name is probably derived from *cryc*, the Old English for a 'staff'. In Old French *criquet* was the name for a bat used in a ball-game. Within a century 'cricket' had become synonymous with 'fair play' and since then anyone accused that their conduct is 'not cricket' receives a stern rebuke that their behaviour is not up to the high standard expected of them.

Daisy cutter

'Daisy cutter' is another cricketing term. A 'cutter' is a type of delivery, bowled at a batsman by the bowler, which strikes the ground on the seam of the cricket ball and then changes direction. A 'daisy cutter' is a different sort of delivery, but equally tricky to deal with. In this case, the ball fails to bounce to the expected height after hitting the ground, perhaps because of an irregularity in the pitch. Instead it continues towards the wicket running very close to, or right along, the ground with the result that it can sometimes take the player batting by surprise, pass under the bat and hit the wicket behind, resulting in a dismissal.

Dark horse

In the world of horse racing, a 'dark horse' is a runner, entered for a race, about which there is little hard information but which seems to have the potential to run well and maybe win. Transferred to people, 'dark horse' is applied to someone whose abilities and likely course of action are unknown.

Dead end

In bowling, the 'end' is one stage in a game: the point at which all bowls have been delivered. A 'dead end' occurs when the jack, or 'target ball', has been driven outside the playing area, known as the 'rink'. When this happens, the 'end' cannot continue and must be replayed. From bowls, a game that has been played for hundreds of years, 'dead end' has passed into everyday speech, to describe the closed end of a passage or thoroughfare, from which there is no exit. It is also used figuratively to describe situations or circumstances which offer no opportunity for progress or development, as in the expression 'dead-end job', meaning one in which an individual sees no prospects of promotion or advancement.

Dead heat

A 'dead heat' is the result of a race in which two or more competitors reach the finishing line at the same time. The sense is similar to that of 'dead end', in that the 'heat' needs to be re-raced if a clear winner is to be found. In practice, of course, this seldom happens and the result is usually recorded as a 'dead-heat' to show that the winners finished equal.

Dead ringer

In American horse racing parlance, 'ringer' has been used since the nineteenth century for a horse illicitly placed in a race as a substitute for another. In the case of a 'dead ringer', the substitute horse is close to being a double of the horse it is replacing; 'dead' in this context is used in the sense of 'exact', as it is in the navigational term 'dead-reckoning. 'Dead ringer' is no longer restricted to horses, however. The phrase is applied to people in circumstances where one person closely resembles another.

Debt of honour

Debts contracted by betting or gambling are not recoverable by legal process and cannot be enforced as binding debts by law. This makes their settlement a matter of honour on the part of the debtor and therefore makes them 'debts of honour'.

Derby

As the 'Blue Riband of the Turf', the Derby is a race for three-year-old colts and fillies held annually on Epsom Downs. It was founded in 1780 and took its name from the 12th Earl of Derby, who one year earlier had established another classic race of the English sporting calendar: the Oaks. The history of the Derby and the pedigree of its competitors has led to the use of 'derby' to describe any competition of particular significance, especially when it has a strong regional significance, as in the expression 'local derby'. In the racing world 'Derby' is now the name given to premier races in many countries.

Do a Bannister

Less common than it was half a century ago, 'doing a Bannister' can be seen as the British equivalent of 'doing a Charley Paddock', in other words making a get-away by running with an exceptional turn of speed. The allusion is to the historic race held in Oxford on 6 May 1954 when Dr Roger Bannister became the first man to run a mile in less than four minutes.

Dominoes

The popular game of dominoes has undergone a strange linguistic metamorphosis. The 'domino' started life as a hooded clerical cloak, which then became a cloak with a half-mask worn at masquerades. The pieces used to play the game of 'dominoes' bear a visual resemblance to both these garments, having a black ebony back and a front through which white pips are revealed, much as the wearer's eyes would have been in the masquerade mask. The practice of arranging 'dominoes' so that they fall in sequence has led to the development of huge elaborate patterns formed by the steady toppling of tens of thousands of carefully positioned coloured 'dominoes'. This in turn has resulted in the phrase 'domino effect', used when one action will inevitably lead to a succession of similar and unstoppable events.

Double-barrelled

A 'double-barrelled' gun is a gun with two barrels, often, but not always, two barrels for firing cartridges filled with shot. From this, a 'double-barrelled' name means a hyphenated surname and a 'double-barrelled' compliment is an ambiguous one which could be interpreted as a criticism or put-down as well as a conventional compliment.

Down and out

George Orwell used this phrase in his 1933 book *Down and Out in Paris and London*, drawing on its popular meaning of being at the end of your resources, with no chance of recovery and only homelessness and grinding poverty to look forward to. This bleak expression comes from the boxing ring, where a boxer who is 'down and out' is technically on the floor and unable to rise in the ten seconds he is allowed to get to his feet again. As a consequence of being 'down and out', he is 'finished', as far as that fight goes, and the contest is awarded to his opponent.

Down the middle

This is an expression borrowed from golf, which is now applied to many situations in which action taken is 'straightforward' and 'uncomplicated' while achieving the result that was wanted. It refers to a ball that finishes in the centre of the fairway of the hole being played.

Drawing a blank

Those who 'draw a blank' fail in what they are trying to achieve. The allusion is to the hunting field where sportsmen would 'draw' a covert to flush out game that might be hiding there. If no game emerged, the draw was a 'blank' and the hunt was obliged to move to another likely location.

Drawing stumps

The act of 'drawing stumps' marks the end of play in a cricket match. The umpires dismantle the wicket, removing the bails and pulling the stumps from the ground. In its abbreviated form this is often referred to simply as 'stumps'. Both expressions are used metaphorically and often in a light-hearted sense to mean reaching the end of something.

Drawing the longbow

In the Middle Ages, British bowmen, particularly Welsh archers, were highly respected for their accuracy and firepower with the longbow. Legends such as those about Robin Hood and his outlaw band were built on stories of exceptional skill at archery. For a time every able-bodied man was expected to practise with the longbow and inevitably some made exaggerated claims about their own prowess. Those who boasted and made false claims were easily shown up when called on to demonstrate their expertise by 'drawing the longbow'. This proved whether or not they were making false claims about their skill as archers and figuratively 'drawing the longbow' still implies that someone is exaggerating.

Duck

This is the ignominious term given to a cricketer who fails to score any runs in an innings. Scoring nought, he or she is said to be 'out for a duck'. The phrase was originally 'out for a duck's egg', which makes the sense a little clearer, because of the resemblance of '0' to a duck's egg. However, 'duck's egg' became abbreviated to 'duck' and the abbreviated expression has passed into the language of cricket. Some score-boards even have a symbol of a duck in profile, which is hung in place after a cricketer is dismissed after leaving the wicket with a score of nought.

Dukes

Why 'dukes' should be the slang for 'fists' is hard to pin down, but expressions like 'put up your dukes' have been common in the lower levels of boxing since the nineteenth century. The most plausible explanation seems to involve rhyming slang, in which 'Duke of Yorks' meant 'forks' and by association 'fingers' and 'hands'. Shortened to 'Dukes' and often pronounced 'Dooks', the phrase was applied to fists.

Entering the lists

In Old English a 'list' was a 'border', 'edging' or 'strip'. By the fourteenth century, 'lists' (in the plural) became the term for the barrier enclosing a space in which jousting, or tilting, took place in medieval tournaments. Any challenger wanting to demonstrate his skill, 'entered the lists' on horseback at the start of a contest with a fellow competitor. Since the days of chivalry, 'entering the lists' has become a general term for embarking on any course of action that is likely to involve rivalry or controversy.

Even money

'Even money' is an expression from horse racing which refers to the odds offered on a particular horse. In this case it implies that the odds offer winnings equal to the amount staked. In a wider context, anything else described as 'even money', or 'evens', has a 'fifty-fifty' chance of success or achieving the desired outcome.

Face-off

As a metaphor, a 'face-off' amounts to a confrontation in which the antagonists square up face to face. The expression is also a technical term in ice hockey and lacrosse, where it refers to the starting or restarting of a game. In ice hockey the puck is dropped between two players (one from each team); the five 'face-off spots' marked on the rink are used for this purpose. In lacrosse, a 'face-off', or 'face', is again conducted between two players. In men's lacrosse both players place their crosses against each other on the ground, with the ball held between the backs of the crosses; in women's lacrosse the crosses are held at waist height, again with the ball between their backs. When the signal is given for play to start, the players in the face-off try to work the ball to the advantage of their own teams.

Fair game

'Fair game' is a term from hunting and shooting that applies to game which can legitimately be hunted in accordance with the Game Laws. The expression is also applied in other situations where individuals are regarded as 'fair game', if it is deemed that they can be fairly teased or made the subject of good-natured banter.

Fall short of

This is another expression taken from archery. Its meaning is self-explanatory and refers to an arrow which fails to reach the target and therefore 'falls short'. In a wider context, to 'fall short' means 'not to come up to standard', as in the more recently coined turn of phrase 'failing to deliver'.

Feathering your oar

Whether you are rowing for recreation or in a competition, 'feathering your oar' reduces wind resistance when it is out of the water. The action takes place as soon as the blade leaves the water. The rower twists the oar through ninety degrees, so that the blade is parallel with the surface while it is being moved into position for the next stroke. Just before that stroke begins, the blade is twisted back to be perpendicular to the surface, so that it will 'catch' the water cleanly when the next stroke is taken.

Fifty cards in a pack

This is a euphemism, coined in America, indicating intellectual shortcomings. A standard pack of cards contains fifty-two cards; so having 'fifty cards in a pack' implies that 'something is missing'; or, one might say, that the pack is 'not all there'.

Follow through

The 'follow through' is an important part of striking the ball in a number of sports, especially golf and cricket. In the 'follow through' the swing is continued after the ball has been hit, to avoid a jerky, mistimed or uncompleted shot. The same meaning is implied when 'follow through' is used in other circumstances in which further action is taken after an initial act, or when action is followed right to the conclusion of an undertaking.

Following suit

In its figurative usage, 'following suit' means to follow someone else's example. The allusion is to card games in which a player plays a card of the suit led by another in the game.

Force the pace

Someone who 'forces the pace' in any activity is trying to increase the speed or tempo, usually by making others work or move faster. The phrase is drawn from running races and horse racing in which one or more competitors begin to break away from the rest of the field by going faster, in the hope that others will tire as they try to keep up.

Forcing one's hand

One of the tactics of many card games is to make another player reveal his or her 'hand' of cards earlier than they would have wished. This is known as 'forcing their hand' and it is a phrase that has been taken up in general usage in the sense of making a person reveal his or her intentions ahead of time.

Frisbee

The light plastic flying disc, which has become a popular throwing toy around the world, was inspired by the pie plates produced by the Frisbie Pie Company of Bridgeport, Connecticut in the late 1950s. Students at nearby Yale University were the first to make full use of the aerodynamic properties of Frisbie Pie plates and by 1957 'frisbees' modelled on them were being produced by the Wham-O-Production Company in California.

From pillar to post

The game of 'real tennis' (described above) gave rise to this expression, which, in general terms, means moving 'from one thing to another' without any clear objective or direction. The analogy is to the flight of a tennis ball in a 'real-tennis' court. Unlike lawn tennis, the ball in this game can strike the walls as well as the floor (as does the ball in a game of squash). However, the walls of a 'real tennis' court contain a number of protrusions which can make the ball fly off in unexpected directions. These resemble 'pillars' and 'posts' in the medieval 'courts' where the game was first played and are now incorporated into the design of all 'real tennis' courts.

Game, set and match

'Game, set and match' is the announcement made after the winning point has been scored in a tennis match. In winning the final game, the victor has also secured the final set and thereby the whole game. Used colloquially, it means a comprehensive win.

Gameplan

'Gameplan' originated in American football as the technical term for a set series of moves and tactics which a team can employ whenever particular objectives need to be achieved. From the football field, 'gameplan' has become widely used on both sides of the Atlantic for a plan of action drawn up for a long-term strategy, such as career development.

Gamesmanship

Stephen Potter helped popularize this expression when it formed the title of his popular 1947 book *The Theory and Practice of Gamesmanship*, which he defined in the sub-title as 'The art of winning games without actually cheating'. 'Gamesmanship' has gained wider currency ever since as a term for achieving success through bending the rules without actually breaking them.

Gentlemen of the Green Baize Road

This was a euphemism for 'whist players' when the game was at the height of its popularity in the nineteenth century. Since 'gentleman of the road' was a euphemism for 'highwaymen', the use of a similar phrase for whist players may have been intended to imply a degree of trickery or 'sharp practice'.

Getting a guernsey

A 'guernsey' is a thick, knitted, fairly closely-fitting sweater originally worn by fishermen. It was also the name given to shirts worn by sportsmen in the nineteenth century and by Australian footballers. It was in Australia that the phrase originated; a footballer who 'got a guernsey' was selected to play for his football team. By association, 'getting a guernsey' developed its additional meaning of 'winning approval', or 'succeeding' in general.

Getting into your stride

The 'stride' is a sporting term found in both athletics and rowing. 'Getting into your stride' carries the general meaning of settling into your optimum work-rate and level of performance. In athletics, it refers to the part of a race following the start, when an athlete settles into his or her racing speed and most comfortable length of stride. Rowing crews settle into their 'stride' after the opening strokes of a race. The initial strokes, which set the boat in motion, are taken at a faster rhythm than the crew's ideal racing speed. Once the boat is moving, the crew deliberately slows the rowing rate on an agreed stroke, in order to settle into a steady and sustainable rhythm for the rest of the race.

Getting your ducks in a row

The impression conveyed in this popular American expression is one of order and organization. The 'ducks' referred to are actually skittles, rather than farmyard fowls, and 'getting your ducks in a row' originally meant setting up your skittles, before it was borrowed to be used in the wider sense of 'having your affairs completed and in order'.

Getting your second wind

After experiencing some breathlessness at the start of a run, athletes warm up and settle into a steady rate of breathing which appears to give an additional burst of energy. This is known as 'second wind' and it is a phrase that is applied to many situations in which individuals recover from a feeling of weariness and discover fresh vigour and energy that enables them to continue their undertakings.

Give and take plate

A 'give and take plate' is a prize awarded in horse racing for runners classified in a particular way. In such races, horses that exceed a standard height carry more than the standard weight and those below that height carry less than the standard weight. This sense of equality reflects the usual meaning of 'give and take' which implies 'fairness' in the exercising of 'understanding' and 'forbearance'.

Giving it your best shot

The 'shot' alluded to in this expression, which came into vogue in the 1980s, is one which strikes a ball, rather than one fired from a gun. The term is particularly appropriate for golfers, who can take time to assess and prepare for their 'shot'. For 'giving it your best shot' has a sense of finality, implying that the 'shot' about to be taken is a crucial one. 'Give it all you've got' has a similar meaning.

Go nap

'Nap' is an abbreviation for the card game named in honour of Napoleon III. In the game, 'Nap' (or 'Napoleon') is the term for the five tricks, which each of the players tries to form. In its figurative sense to 'go nap' means 'risking all you have' on a venture by backing it to the hilt.

Going down like ninepins

'Ninepins' is another name for the traditional game of 'skittles' in which nine skittles are arranged in a pattern and players take turns in rolling a ball to knock them over, scoring a point for each one that 'goes down'. Early forms of 'skittles' date from hundreds of years ago and throughout its history the game has always been popular. At various times attempts were made to ban it on the grounds that it was a distraction from more valuable pastimes, such as archery practice. This popularity may have had a part to play in the expression 'going down like ninepins' which implies that people or objects are 'going down' in large numbers. When gambling on 'ninepins' threatened to become a problem, all form of skittles were banned in London. By 1840 gambling on skittles had become so serious that certain American states also banned the game. This led to the creation of 'tenpin' bowling which got round the ban by the addition of an extra pin.

Going for gold

Although gold medals had been awarded to winning competitors for at least a hundred years, it was not until the 1980 Winter Olympics that 'going for gold' was taken up as a popular exclamation meaning 'aiming for the highest achievement'. It seems that the American Olympic team were the first to be urged to 'go for gold', though the phrase and the desire quickly spread throughout the whole Olympic community and now 'going for gold' is a popular expression of determination and a willingness to succeed.

Going the distance

Boxers who manage to fight through all the rounds of a contest until the final bell are said to have 'gone the distance'. Even those who do not actually win still have the satisfaction and sense of achievement which comes from lasting up to fifteen three-minute rounds with an equally matched opponent. The same sense of endurance is applied to other activities in which one can be described as to have 'gone the distance', that is to say stuck at a task and completed it once it has been started.

Good innings

A 'good innings' is a metaphor applied to both men and women for those who have recently died, but who have had a good, and frequently, long life. The allusion is to an 'innings' in cricket, the period in which a player is at the wicket and able to score runs.

Good run for your money

There is something pleasing about having a 'good run for your money'. In contests of all types, a worthy opponent can give 'a good run for your money' which makes victory all the more enjoyable. A successful return for hard work and effort is similarly a 'good run for your money'. So is the enjoyment derived from any activity. The 'run' alluded to in the phrase is a horse race; in this case one in which a backed horse provides plenty of excitement for those who have placed bets on it, even if it does not win.

Grand slam

In bridge, winning all the tricks in a deal is known as a 'Grand slam'. In tennis the phrase is used in a similar sense when a player holds, at the same time, all four of the world's major singles titles from the championships in Australia, France, England and the USA.

Great hit

Associations with 'hit' songs and 'hits' in other areas of popular culture might lead to the conclusion that a 'great hit' is a recently coined expression. However, it derives from an old board game, 'hit and miss', as well as from the equally old game 'backgammon'. A 'great hit' amounts to a 'stroke of good luck' or a 'great success' and alludes to scoring a 'hit' in either of the games; in backgammon two 'hits' equal a 'gammon'.

Hat trick

A run of three consecutive successes in a number of sports (and some non-sporting activities) is now referred to as a 'hat trick', although the phrase originated in cricket. In order to get a 'hat trick', a bowler must dismiss three batsmen with three consecutive deliveries. In the past it was customary for a bowler who achieved this to receive a hat provided by his club.

Having an ace up your sleeve

These days 'having an ace up your sleeve' is regarded as something to be proud of. It implies a high level of planning and preparation, which has equipped you with a secret resource that you can use to your advantage when the need arises. However, the expression originated in card games when 'having an ace up your sleeve' identified you as a cheat and someone who was prepared to gain an unfair advantage over other players by hiding a high-scoring card in your clothing, which you could secretly substitute for another to create a winning hand.

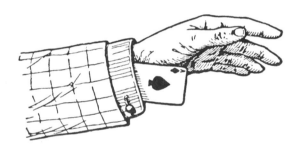

Having no legs

This is an expression applied to a golf stroke, or some other sporting activity, in which a player fails to achieve an anticipated distance by his 'shot'. The allusion is to a runner, whose legs become too tired to continue racing. So a golf ball that 'has no legs' does not have the power from the stroke to carry it to the point the golfer was aiming for.

Having the bit between your teeth

The purpose of the 'bit' in a horse's bridle is to provide the rider with a means of controlling the animal. The word is derived from the Old English word for 'bite', which conveys the sense that the 'bit' is the mouth-piece of the bridle. When a horse is being ridden normally, the bit presses against the soft part of its mouth whenever the rider pulls on the reins. However, if a horse grabs it, so that 'the bit is between its teeth', pulling on the reins has no effect and the rider loses control. In its figurative sense, 'having the bit between your teeth' means 'becoming self-willed', though, in a more positive light, it can also mean 'to act with determination'.

Having the game in your hands

To 'have the game in your hands' means to be confident of winning and alludes to a 'hand' of cards which you are convinced will win the game.

Hazard

The modern meaning usually applied to a 'hazard' is that of something 'posing a danger'. However, when the word was first recorded in the thirteenth century its meaning alluded to a different sort of chance. 'Hazard' was the name for a dice game (as it still is). Later the word was applied to openings in a 'real tennis' court, through which players could try to hit the ball in order to score points, and to a winning shot in billiards. In all its meanings a sense of chance or risk is involved.

Hedging your bets

People who metaphorically 'hedge their bets' seek to protect themselves from loss or changes of fortune; the expression has the additional meaning of 'equivocating'. In horse racing 'hedging your bets' means to protect yourself against losses by cross-betting on other horses in the race, whose 'placing' at the finish would provide a degree of compensation.

Heptathlon

Taking its inspiration from the pentathlon, the five-event competition of the ancient Olympic Games, the 'heptathlon' is a modern, seven-event competition, principally for women. It was first officially recognized in 1981 and now forms part of the worldwide athletics calendar. 'Heptathlon' events are held over two days during which 'heptathletes' compete in: the 100-metres hurdles, high jump, shot put, 200-metre run, long jump, javelin throw and 800-metre run. The winner is the competitor with the highest aggregate score from all seven events.

Here's mud in your eye

This is a popular toast offered casually these days to a group of friends or acquaintances. However, when it was first coined it had a somewhat ambivalent meaning. In racing circles 'mud in your eye' implied that you were behind the leading the horse and therefore liable to be hit by mud thrown from its hooves. The only rider without 'mud in the eye' would be the one on the leading horse. Therefore offering the toast of 'Here's mud in your eye', invites others to drink to your success and, by implication, their own failure to finish ahead of you.

Hit for six

In a game of cricket, six runs are scored if the ball is hit over the boundary without touching the ground after leaving the bat. 'Hitting a six' is comparatively rare and implies that the player achieving it has complete mastery over the bowling. When the expression is applied to other situations, anything 'hit for six' is totally defeated. In the same sense, being 'hit for six' means being 'completely astonished' by what has happened.

Holding all the cards

Here again playing card games provide the point of reference for this well-known expression. Any player 'holding all the cards', in other words holding the best cards, will determine the outcome of the game. So, in a general sense, 'holding all the cards' means to be in a position of control over other people as well as a situation.

Hook, line and sinker

Anyone who swallows a story 'hook, line and sinker' shows that he or she is as gullible as a greedy fish which swallows the lead weight and part of the fishing line as well as the baited hook.

In a brace of shakes

Doing something 'in a brace of shakes' means doing it instantly. The reference to 'shakes' links the expression with playing dice and doing something 'in a brace of shakes' is as quick as it takes to 'shake the dice box twice'.

In at the kill

The hunting field provides the origin for this expression which is now used largely in its metaphorical sense. Huntsmen or hunt followers who are 'in at the kill' are present when the fox (or other quarry) is caught and killed. That is to say, they have kept with the hounds from the moment the pack picked up the fox's scent. Used figuratively, to be 'in at the kill' means to be present at the end of something.

In full cry

Hunting again provides the source for this expression which is actually the precursor to being 'in at the kill'. When a pack of hounds detects the scent of their quarry, they give 'full cry', barking and yelping as they set off in pursuit. Applied to humans, 'in full cry' has the same meaning. When someone, or a group of people set off in hot pursuit of an objective, they are often described as being 'in full cry'.

In spades

This is a phrase that is usually used to infer that something has been done to 'a great extent', as in a statement such as 'He repaid our hospitality in spades'. The reference to 'spades' comes from those card games in which spades are the highest ranking suit.

In the bag

Anything regarded as being 'in the bag' is as 'good as certain', probably by association with the bag in which a hunter placed his game when it had been killed. However, the phrase has a contradictory meaning in Australia, where it is used in racing circles. If a horse is described as being 'in the bag' the meaning is that it will not be running in the race for which it was entered.

In the running

Here is another term for the actual race in which horses compete. A horse 'in the running' is up among the main body of the field, close enough to the leader to have a chance of winning the race. On the other hand one that is 'out of the running' has been removed from the race even before it got under way. Both turns of phrase are used in other contexts, particularly political ones where candidates are described as being 'in the running' if they still have a chance of being elected, while those 'out of the running' have to reconcile themselves to losing even before the election takes place.

In the swim

People 'in the swim' are in the main 'current' of life and are well placed to further their social standing. The expression comes from angling in which a 'swim' is the term given to a shoal of fish. If an angler is able to cast his bait 'in the swim' he is likely to have a good catch.

Into the final straight

The concluding part of many races, including those involving motor vehicles and horses, as well as athletes, takes place over a straight length of track. This is often the most exciting part of the race as competitors push themselves to overtake the leader and cross the finishing line first. Excitement and a sense of uncertainty has led to 'into the final straight' being applied to 'races' far removed from sporting tracks and arenas. The closing days of election campaigns are sometimes referred to in these terms, with politicians and political parties making their last efforts to win votes as they come 'into the final straight' before polling day.

Jackpot

Lotteries, 'one-armed bandits' and other forms of gambling build up a pool of money from a large number of players, so that one (or at the most a very few) fortunate winners can share the 'jackpot'. The word is derived from another gambling game: poker. Here the 'jackpot' is a pot which can only be opened once a player has a pair of jacks or better.

Jockey

Since the seventeenth century 'jockey' has been the name given to professional riders in horse-races. It appears to have derived from the Scottish first name 'Jock', which is a Scots variant of 'Jack'. A 'jockey' was a 'little Jack', a term often used in the same way as 'lad'.

Jodhpurs

These riding breeches, close-fitting from knee to ankle, take their name from a nineteenth-century Indian state. In the 1860s one of the leading polo players in India was the Maharajah of Jodhpur, in western India. When he played polo, he wore riding breeches that were tight at the ankle. British officers with whom he played adopted his polo attire and brought them back home to Britain where they became popular riding-wear.

Jumping the gun

For many years firing a gun has been the signal to start running races. A competitor who 'jumps the gun' starts running just before the gun is fired. In athletics this results in a false start and the race is restarted. However, 'jumping the gun' occurs elsewhere and in general it means that an individual or organization starts before an agreed time, in the hope of gaining an advantage over competitors.

Keeping the ball rolling

As a popular metaphor from ball games, 'keeping the ball rolling' means maintaining the momentum of an activity: a conversation, entertainment, a game, or a debate. People who 'keep the ball rolling' take the initiative in preventing interest from flagging, just as players in ball games like hockey or football, keep the game moving by 'keeping the ball rolling'.

Keeping up your guard

Boxing is the sport which provides these words of cautionary advice. A boxer's 'guard' is the defensive posture in which he holds his body, arms and gloves. 'Keeping up his guard' ensures that he is always protected as well as he can be from punches thrown by his opponent. The opposite posture is known as 'dropping your guard'. In the boxing ring, a boxer who 'drops his guard', lowers his gloves, leaving himself exposed to blows from his opponent. Outside the boxing ring 'keeping up your guard' implies that your are 'vigilant' and 'wary', constantly on the look-out for the unexpected and well prepared to cope with it.

Keeping your cards close to your chest

This is the behaviour of a cautious person who wants to keep his or her secrets hidden. The allusion is to games of cards in which players 'keep their cards close to their chests' to guard them jealously from the gaze of others.

Kick into touch

'Kicking into touch' is a metaphor from football (soccer); 'touch' being an abbreviation for the 'touch-line': the line marking each side of the field of play. A ball 'kicked into touch' goes out of play, which supplies the meaning of the metaphorical sense; an idea or a proposition which is 'kicked into touch' is removed from further discussion. In football a 'kick into touch' can be a deliberate action, rather than an error. If a member of one team is injured and play continues, it is common for a player of the opposing team deliberately to 'kick the ball into touch' allowing play to stop while the injured player receives treatment.

Kicking up a shindy

'Shindy' is a variation in spelling of 'shinty', a game of Scottish origin which resembles hockey. Its name may be derived from cries used in the game: 'shin ye, shin you' and 'shin to you'. By the eighteenth century, 'Shindy' was one of the names by which the game was known, but its use in 'kicking up a shindy' dates from the nineteenth century, when 'shindy' drew on the alternative meaning of a 'commotion' or 'disturbance', which is probably associated with the excitement generated by playing the game.

Kick-off

Many different games begin with a 'kick-off', the action by one side which literally 'starts the ball rolling'. The term has been widely used for the start of other activities involving a group of people in which all may participate. In a meeting, for example, one of those present might be invited to 'kick off' a discussion by being the first to speak.

Kingpin

The reference to 'pin' in this expression gives a clue to its origin in the game of skittles. Among the nine pins set up as the 'target', the 'kingpin' is either the one in the centre of the formation, or the one at the apex. In both cases, knocking over the 'kingpin' usually means that all the other skittles will be knocked down as well. In its figurative sense a 'kingpin' refers to the principal person in any group or undertaking.

Kit

'Kit' is a general word for essential equipment used in various activities. Soldiers refer to their uniform and field equipment as 'kit', which the military 'kitbag' was designed to contain. In the sporting arena, 'kit' takes the form of clothing, protective gear and equipment used by participants, who also carry their 'kit' in a different form of 'kitbag'. 'Kit' was known in English by the eighteenth century and probably came about as an abbreviation of the Dutch *kitte*, which was a circular wooden vessel bound with hoops in which tools and other items of equipment were kept.

Kitty

In games where players have the chance to win money, a common fund representing the winnings is often known as the 'kitty'. The origin of this is the same as that of 'kit' (above). Instead of tools or other equipment, the 'kitty' contained money. In the case of games played in public houses, the 'kitty' might well have been a tankard in which the participants placed their share of the winnings, for the Dutch word *kit* meant a 'tankard'.

Knock spots off

'Knocking the spots off' someone means to 'beat them soundly' and 'easily get the better of them'. The allusion is to demonstrating a high level of skill at shooting. In the late nineteenth century, skilled marksmen, with both pistols and rifles, used to display their expertise by shooting at playing cards, with the aim of 'knocking out the spots' or pips. Only the best shots were able to do this and their success set them far above less accomplished ones.

Knockout

A 'knockout' can refer to a blow on the head which renders someone unconscious; it can mean that an individual or a team has been eliminated from a sporting competition as a result of being defeated by another; and it is used colloquially as an expression of astonishment. In each case 'knockout' stems from the boxing ring, where it is the term used when a boxer strikes his opponent with such effect that he is knocked to the floor and is unable to get to his feet, to carry on fighting, within the ten seconds allowed by the rules and counted by the referee.

Knowing a hawk from a handsaw

Shakespeare gives Hamlet this curious expression when he is talking to his former university friends, Rosencrantz and Guildenstern, 'I am but mad north-north-west;' the prince tells them, 'when the wind is southerly, I know a hawk from a handsaw.' Four hundred years later, his words appear to confirm Hamlet's madness. However, Elizabethan audiences would have recognized through his use of these words that the prince was only pretending to be mad. The allusion he draws is from the sport of falconry. The 'hawk' referred to is evidently the bird of prey used to catch game. The 'handsaw' has nothing to do with carpentry. In this case it is more than likely a corruption of 'hernshaw', or 'heronsew', a 'young heron.' So, by telling his friends that he can distinguish between a bird of prey and its quarry, Hamlet implies that he is sane enough to know one thing from another; in other words to know what is really going on around him.

Knowing the ropes

Aboard a sailing ship 'knowing the ropes' implied that you knew which rope was attached to which sail and therefore had a full working knowledge of the ship and its rigging. The expression also has reference to the boxing ring, where a boxer who 'knows the ropes' has an instinctive understanding of where in the ring he is in relation to the ropes surrounding it. 'Knowing the ropes' is essential to avoid allowing oneself to be backed into a corner by an opponent. In general usage 'knowing the ropes' implies an understanding of what needs to be done gained from experience of having done it before.

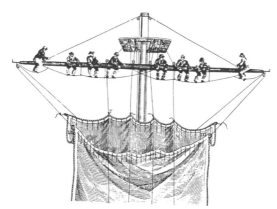

Lacrosse

The game which is known as 'lacrosse' today, was brought to Europe in the eighteenth century by an early French missionary in Canada. While he was exploring the area around the St Lawrence River, François-Xavier de Charlevoix discovered a game played by local Indians which they called *baggataway*. This was played using a form of hockey stick, which resembled a shepherd's crook, or *crosse* in French. De Charlevoix called the game *le jeu de la crosse* ('the game of the cross') which in due course was abbreviated to 'lacrosse'.

Last lap

Like the 'final straight' (above), the 'last lap' is the concluding part of a race, usually of middle-distance or longer. Runners entering the last lap traditionally hear the ringing of a bell to indicate that they are starting the final circuit of the race. Here tactics and stamina come together to produce a finishing burst of running which, hopefully, will win the race. The 'last lap'; is used metaphorically to mean 'the beginning of the end', the point at which 'light can be seen at the end of the tunnel'.

Laying an egg

Given that a score of nought in cricket is called a 'duck' (above), originally a 'duck's egg', 'laying an egg' is the process that produces a score of nought. Baseball makes use of 'goose egg' in the same sense as 'duck's egg' in cricket and 'laying an egg' occurs on both sides of the Atlantic to mean a 'failure' or 'flop'.

Leading card

Players in card games invariably lead with their strongest suit, which contains their 'leading cards'. By analogy, a 'leading card' in any other context is the strongest position a person, or a group of people, holds. Whether that is the most telling point in an argument, or the principal performer in a production, both count as 'leading cards'.

League table

'League tables' were originally drawn up in the sporting world to show the relative positions of teams, or individual sportsmen and women, in a variety of competitive sports. In the 1990s, 'league tables' entered public life in a wider sense, when official statistics were used to compile 'league tables' showing (and more controversially comparing) the performance of institutions in areas of public interest, such as education and health.

Left in the lurch

Anyone 'left in the lurch' regards themselves as having been abandoned in an awkward predicament. 'Left in the lurch' was originally a term from the game of cribbage. It applies to the situation in which one player's pegs reach a total of sixty-one before the other's have passed thirty-one.

Level pegging

'Level pegging' is another scoring term from cribbage. In this case the players' scores are equal and the pegs are side by side, as they match each other move for move. In its wider usage, 'level pegging' means that two people are evenly matched in their abilities and achievements.

Level playing field

The image of a 'level playing field' as a sphere of activity in which no one side is disadvantaged developed during the 1980s. References to 'level playing fields' became popular in politics and business as an indication of even-handedness, in which all those with an interest in a subject were able to participate on an equal footing.

Loading the dice

'Loaded dice' are dice which have been illegally weighted, so that they fall with the required face up. Therefore 'loading the dice' is an act designed to gain advantage over an opponent. The term is used in expressions like 'loading the dice against' someone, which means prejudicing their chances of success.

Long odds

In horse racing, 'odds' is the term applied to a betting quotation indicating the amount to be paid if a horse wins a race or is placed in the first three. The 'odds' quoted amount to a ratio between the amounts staked by both parties to the bet. 'Long odds' implies that there is a large difference between the amounts staked, as would be the case with 'odds' of, say, 100:1. The longer the 'odds', the greater is the element of risk and correspondingly the size of any reward. With 'short odds' the risk is significantly reduced, the ratio of the amounts staked is closer and the return on a win is comparatively low.

Love

Tennis and several other ball and racket games include 'love' in their scoring terminology to represent 'nil'. In this context 'love' has no connection with affairs of the heart. It is actually a pun on the French *l'oeuf*, meaning 'the egg', which in shape originally resembled the zero of 'nil'. The usage here is similar to that of 'duck's egg' in cricket and 'goose's egg' in baseball.

Main chance

The centuries old dice game of 'hazard' has provided this euphemism for 'profit' or 'money'. In a game of hazard, 'main' and 'chance' refer to different throws of the dice. When all stakes have been placed, the first player (known as the 'caster') throws the dice to establish a 'main' point, which has to be 5, 6, 7, 8, or 9. If he or she is successful, the 'caster' throws the dice again to establish a 'chance' point. This must total 4, 5, 6, 7, 8, 9, or 10, but it must not be the same number as the 'main' point number. Some numbers forming a 'chance' point win the stake money out right. Others require the 'caster' to throw the dice a third time, after which he or she may or may not win the money, depending on the number thrown.

Making first base

In baseball, 'making first base' means successfully reaching the first stage in scoring a 'run'. It is an expression widely used in North America to indicate a positive beginning. 'Making first base' in a piece of work means completing the initial stage, and among teenagers 'first base' is a euphemism for a first kiss, the initial stage of a romantic encounter.

Making the running

The horse which 'makes the running' in a horse race is the one that takes the lead. It may not necessarily be the winner, but in going to the front it 'sets the pace' that the others must keep if they are to stand a chance of winning themselves. The phrase is used in other situations as well. Athletes can 'make the running', so can businesses and individuals. All share the common attribute of 'hitting the front' and making others quicken their pace if they are to keep up.

Marathon

When the modern Olympic Games were begun in 1896 the 'marathon' was included as one of the events. As a long-distance running race, it had a suitably ancient pedigree. The name and the race recall the Battle of Marathon fought in 490 B.C. This was a decisive battle between the Athenians and the Persians, which established the course of European history thereafter, and from which the Athenian army emerged victorious. News of the victory reached Athens by way of a runner who covered the twenty-three miles at such speed that he died having delivered his message. After the 'marathon' became an established Olympic event, the distance was standardized at 26 miles 385 yards (45.052 kilometres) and from the Olympics 'marathons' have spread worldwide as popular events in which thousands of competitors take part. The stamina and will-power required to run such a distance has led to 'marathon' being applied to any feat requiring great endurance.

Miss the mark

In archery, the 'mark' is an aiming point used by an archer. This is calculated to enable the arrow to hit the target, allowing for wind conditions and range. Arrows that fail to hit the target are reckoned to have 'missed the mark'. In its broader usage 'missing the mark' carries the same sense into any situation in which an objective is missed through miscalculation and possibly poor direction.

Moving the goalposts

Football has supplied a number of metaphors which have become widely used in recent years, of which 'moving the goalposts' is one of the most vivid and popular. The 'goalposts' are used figuratively for 'established conditions', recognized and agreed by all participants in an undertaking, which are 'moved' or amended once the undertaking has been commenced. The implication in the expression is that significant alterations are made to previously agreed terms, often with the underlying suspicion that the changes are designed to disadvantage one of the participants.

Neck and neck

A 'neck' is one of the officially recognized measures used in horse racing to estimate distance between runners; the others are 'nose', 'head', 'length' and 'distance'. When horses are described as being 'neck and neck' they are very close together indeed, virtually side-by-side. This is the meaning when 'neck and neck' is applied to similar situations when 'contenders' have little to show between them, whether they are being judged academically, physically or in some other sphere of human endeavour.

Neither a hawk nor a buzzard

As falconry developed during the Middle Ages, the sport acquired a hierarchy of its own which mirrored that in society. Certain birds of prey were restricted to certain social classes and only members of a particular class were entitled to hunt with the hawk allotted to it. With this in mind, the origin of 'neither a hawk nor a buzzard' becomes clearer. 'Hawks' in general were hunting birds, trained and kept at great expense by those with the means and time to enjoy falconry. The buzzard, on the other hand, was regarded as a lowly bird of prey. So anyone described as 'neither a hawk nor a buzzard' was regarded as being of a doubtful social status. Such a person was neither a servant, nor a member of the gentry.

Nice guys finish last

This jaundiced maxim for the way life works out was coined by Leo Durocher, who was a baseball manager in the late 1940s and early 1950s. Speaking of a rival team, the New York Giants, he told reporters that they were 'All nice guys. They'll finish last. Nice guys. Finish last.' Durocher used the same ruthless turn of phrase as the title for his autobiography.

Not in my book

The 'book' alluded to in this expression is a gambling 'book' in which records are kept of all bets made. The 'book' is therefore a definitive record and used in its metaphorical sense it amounts to 'the last word' on a subject. Anything that is 'not in my book' does not accord with 'my view of things'.

Not playing with a full deck

The meaning of this expression is similar to that of 'fifty cards in a pack' (above), which itself is not a 'full deck'. 'Not playing with a full deck' is, therefore, another euphemism for being 'not all there', or displaying obvious intellectual shortcomings.

Off one's own bat

Cricket again supplies this expression for personal endeavour. Anything achieved 'off one's own bat' is accomplished through your own efforts and on your own initiative. The reference is to the player batting at the wicket who can only rely on his or her own skill with the bat to score runs. A ball hit 'off one's bat' carries a feeling of satisfaction, which translates aptly into other activities in which individuals are called on to act independently of others.

Off your game

This is a general expression applied to people who are not performing to their usual standard. It arises, self-evidently, from the sporting world where players who are 'off their game' are missing shots or failing to play as well as they usually do.

On a sticky wicket

Weather conditions play an important part in games of cricket, especially those in the British Isles. Given that the ball is almost always bowled so that it bounces on the wicket before reaching the player who is batting, the condition of the wicket is of vital importance in deciding what tactics to employ. A 'sticky wicket' is one of the most hazardous to play on. Rain-soaked, but fast-drying, it can make the ball cut sharply to one side and rise abruptly. Batting on a 'sticky wicket' requires concentration and skill to avoid accidentally mistiming a stroke and thereby presenting a catch to the fielding side, or allowing the ball to hit the wicket. The phrase is used less frequently away from the cricket field than it once was. However, its wider meaning remains the same, implying that care and vigilance are needed in dealing with an awkward and unpredictable situation.

On the back foot

A boxer who is in control of his fighting leads with the front foot, on which his weight is placed when he lands his punches. However, if his opponent begins to get the upper hand and lands a succession of telling punches, the first boxer may be forced to retreat 'on the back foot'. This is the meaning given to the expression when it is applied elsewhere. To be forced 'onto the back foot' means that you have to adopt a defensive posture, from which it is difficult to launch a counter-attack.

On the ball

Success in any ball game depends on keeping your eye 'on the ball'. This applies to field games like hockey and football as much as it does to racket games such as tennis and squash. Therefore anyone said to be 'on the ball' is 'alert' and 'in control' of whatever they are engaged in.

On the cards

This expression comes from the use of playing cards in fortune telling. In this connection it casts either a favourable or unfavourable light on what might be predicted, depending on the circumstances; for anything described as being 'on the cards' is regarded as being likely to happen.

On the ropes

A boxing ring is formed by three linen-covered ropes, placed one above the other in a parallel formation and held taut by four padded corner posts. Part of a boxer's skill is to move around the ring, dodging punches thrown by his opponent while landing punches of his own. Aside from being knocked to the floor, the situation he seeks most to avoid is being pinned against or 'on the ropes' by the force of his opponent's punches. If this happens, a boxer has less opportunity to land effective blows of his own and he is also unable to move away from the onslaught to regain his attacking stance. To be 'on the ropes', then, amounts to being forced back to the point where you are close to being beaten – a situation which can arise in any number of circumstances.

On your tod

This phrase, meaning 'on your own' appears to have little, if no connection, with either sports or games. However, when rhyming slang is introduced, the explanation and association is revealed. 'On your tod' is an abbreviated form of 'on your Tod Sloan' ('Sloan' rhyming with 'alone'). And the sporting connection? Tod Sloane was a famous American jockey. He died in 1933 and the expression was recorded from the following year.

One-horse race

When there is a clear favourite in a horse race, with such an impressive record that none of the other runners stand a chance of beating it, the event is described as a one-horse race. The same turn of phrase is applied to other situations in which one competitor is certain to win. Appointments to jobs or other important positions, elections and athletic events can all be described as 'one-horse' races if there is an outright 'winner' before the event even begins.

Outbox

The reference to boxing is clear in this expression. If one boxer is said to 'outbox' his opponent, he displays superior boxing skill. This implicit superiority is transferred to other 'contests' in which to 'outbox' someone or something is used metaphorically to mean that they have beaten the opponent by a greater degree of expertise, coupled with 'power' and 'agility'.

Outsider

An 'outsider' in horse racing circles is a horse assessed as having very little chance of winning. In the same way, the term is used metaphorically when it is applied to people or organizations entering a contest of some description with little likelihood of beating other contenders.

Over the moon

As one of the most common modern clichés to express 'rapturous delight', 'over the moon' has been in use for a surprisingly long time. There are references to it dating from the nineteenth-century diaries of society ladies, but it probably achieved its first wave of popularity in the well-known eighteenth-century nursery rhyme,

> Hey diddle diddle
> The cat and the fiddle,
> The cow jumped over the moon.

During the 1980s it was used by football players and managers to express pleasure after a successful game. Not long after that it was being pilloried by some sections of the media. But twenty years on, 'over the moon' is still heard when people are excited and happy about something that has happened to them.

Overshoot the mark

'The mark' referred to here is the same as that in 'miss the mark'. It is a term in archery for an aiming point, which an archer calculates will enable an arrow to hit the target, taking into consideration range and wind direction. Therefore, an arrow which 'overshoots the mark' flies past the target. In the same sense, any other action which 'overshoots the mark' goes beyond what was intended.

Over the odds

This is another reference to the 'odds' applied in betting on horse races. Here, though, the phrase is used more often away from the race-course than in connection with it. Something that is 'over the odds' is reckoned to be 'higher than usual'. It is often used in a financial context, in expressions such as 'He paid over the odds for it', meaning that someone paid more than usual for whatever was bought.

Par

In Latin *par* means 'equal' and the same word is used in English with the same meaning in expressions like 'on a par with'. In golf, 'par' has a specific meaning. Each golf-course (and each hole on it) is assessed by means of a standardized system, to determine how many strokes a good player would be expected to take under normal playing conditions. The number arrived at is referred to as 'par'. Players who complete the hole or the round in a fewer number of strokes score 'below par', those with a higher number of strokes score 'above par'.

Parry

'Parry' is a term from fencing which has entered the language with the same meaning of 'averting', or 'turning aside an attack', whether literal or metaphorical. Like much fencing terminology, 'parry' is derived from French, where the verb *parer* means to 'ward off' and 'avoid'. In fencing a 'parry' is a defensive action which deflects the attacker's blade.

Passing the buck

These days, 'passing the buck' means evading responsibility or shifting blame onto other people. When the phrase was coined in the nineteenth century, however, it had a different emphasis. In some card games a marker, known as a 'buck, was placed in front of the dealer to show who the dealer was. When it was someone else's turn to deal, the 'buck' was passed. Originally the 'buck' may have been a piece of buck-shot, or possibly a silver dollar, which was passed from dealer to dealer.

Peg away

The presence of 'peg' alerts one to a connection with the game of cribbage, in which players' scores are shown by the position of pegs placed in a cribbage board. Players build up their scores by moving their pegs steadily round the board, a process which gave rise to this expression. 'Pegging away' implies steady, persistent application to a task, often in the face of set-backs.

Peg out

This is another commonly used expression that originated in cribbage. 'Peg out' is a well-established euphemism meaning 'to die'. First applied to death in humans and animals, it has also been applied to mechanical 'death' in expressions like, 'My moped pegged out and I had to walk the rest of the way'. The allusion is to the end of a game of cribbage when a player 'pegs out' the last holes.

Pell-mell

Anything undertaken 'pell-mell' is approached headlong, in a state of reckless confusion. This definition is a far cry from the calm order of two of London's most famous thoroughfares, but both Pall Mall and the Mall in St James's Park are connected with the phrase. The link between them is the old game of 'pall-mall' (sometimes 'pell-mell') which was popular at the court of Charles II. This originated in Italy as a game somewhat like croquet with the name *pallo a maglio* ('ball to mallet'). It was very popular in France, as was noted in an account from 1621 which stated, 'A paille mall is a wooden hammer set to the end of a long staff to strike a boule with, at which game noblemen and gentlemen in France doe play much'. The game was brought to England by the Stuart kings and became so popular that Charles II had a new 'mall alley' built in St James's Park in 1660. This was about half a mile long, fenced, with a double row

of trees on either side. Samuel Pepys recorded in his diary that the surface of the 'mall' was carefully prepared with powdered cockle shells to maintain a fast surface for the balls as they flew towards the iron hoops through which they had to pass. Presumably 'pell-mell' became an apt description for the enthusiasm with which players applied themselves to the game.

Pepper game

A pre-game warm-up in baseball is known as a 'pepper game', in which a batter strikes balls thrown by fielders around the playing area.

Photo-finish

The development of high-speed photography led to the use of cameras to determine very close finishes in various types of race. Special cameras are mounted at the finish to photograph competitors and runners as they cross the finish line. When the end of a race is very close, the photograph is often the only way of being certain who has won. This technology gave rise to 'photo-finish' which is used figuratively to describe the end of any contest in which contenders are neck and neck as they come to the line.

Pinch-hitter

'Pinch-hitter' is a term from baseball used to describe a player who always hits the ball hard. 'Pinch-hitters' are put in to bat when their teams are up against it and need runs. From this, 'pinch-hitter' has developed its meaning by being applied to anyone who takes the place of another in a crisis.

Ping-Pong

The earliest references to 'Ping-Pong' as an alternative name for table tennis date from the end of the nineteenth century. James Gibb, a former Cambridge University cross-country athlete and holder of the four-mile record, had the idea of creating a family game using a celluloid toy ball he had bought on a trip to America. Using a hollow vellum racket, he devised a game which amounted to a form of indoor, table-top tennis. The name of the game was registered as 'Ping-Pong' from the sound made by the ball first bouncing on a table and then being hit by the bat.

Pipped at the post

A competitor who is 'pipped at the post' is beaten with victory in sight. The 'post' is evidently the finishing post, but 'pipped' is less easy to explain in this context. It appears to be associated with the sense of 'defeat' that comes from the term 'blackballed', the black ball being alluded to as a 'pip'. The term comes from secret ballots, in which members of clubs and societies cast votes, on the eligibility of prospective members, using coloured balls to indicate their preferences. A member who wanted to vote against someone used a black ball, and so 'blackballed' became a term meaning 'defeated'.

Pitch and toss

This is an old gambling game in which coins are 'pitched' at a mark. The player whose coin lands nearest the mark has the right to toss into the air all the other's coins and is allowed to keep the ones which land 'heads up'. From the decidedly risky nature of this game, 'to play pitch and toss' has come to mean 'gambling recklessly' with your assets.

Playing for time

The end of a cricket match does not necessarily mean victory for one team and defeat for the other. In cricket, a 'draw' is a third outcome and this can be achieved by a team which uses appropriate tactics and so avoids defeat. In order to do this the team must keep batting until time runs out. Hence the expression 'playing for time', which implies that the batting team have given up 'playing for runs', opting instead to bat cautiously and defensively in order to avoid losing wickets and therefore continue batting until the end of the game. As a metaphor, 'playing for time' implies applying similar delaying tactics, to stave off defeat or failure in other activities.

Playing fast and loose

The original way to 'play fast and loose' was at a fairground, where 'fast and loose' was a game in which unsuspecting victims were persuaded to bet that they could pin a folded belt to a board by passing a skewer through a loop formed in it. However, unknown to them, the trickster running the stall folded the belt in such a way that pinning it to the board was virtually impossible. Invariably, when the belt was pulled away, it was shown not to be 'fast', but 'loose', so the victim lost his bet. Since then 'playing fast and loose' has come to imply a certain deviousness and trickery about someone's conduct and actions.

Plus fours

'Plus fours' became popular during the 1920s as a style of loose trousers with the legs gathered on to bands and finishing just below the knee, which allowed great freedom of movement for outdoor sports, such as golf. They acquired their name from the additional four inches of cloth which was required to allow fullness at the knee before being tucked into long heavy socks.

Point blank

In French, *point blanc* ('white mark') is the bull's-eye of an archery target. To be sure of hitting this, an archer needed to fire from a fairly close range, sighting the line of his arrow straight at the centre of the target. From archery the expression has broadened in its application and is now used with reference to anything that is struck or hit from a very close range.

Point to point

A 'point-to-point' is a horse race restricted to amateur riders. The horses too are not full time racehorses and to prove this owners and riders supply proof that they have been regularly and fairly hunted with a recognized pack of hounds. In racing parlance, a 'point-to-point' is, as its name suggests, a race from one point to another. As such it is classified as a 'steeplechase', a form of cross-country race in which horses and riders have to negotiate a number of obstacles. 'Steeplechases' were originally raced over fields, ditches, hedges and any other obstacles that the runners encountered; these days they are run over prepared courses. The idea of a steeplechase appears to have been developed in Ireland where, early in the nineteenth century, a hunting party decided to race each other in a straight line towards a distant steeple.

Pulling a fast one

'Pulling a fast one' generally implies that some underhand method has been used to deceive and possibly cheat another person. However, when the phrase was coined in cricket it represented a perfectly legitimate ploy used by bowlers. Changing the speed at which a ball is bowled is one way of confusing the player batting at the other end and possibly catching him or her unawares. Bowlers who vary the pace of their deliveries, as well as their direction, are more likely to take wickets than those whose bowling becomes predictable. So, 'pulling a fast one' in a cricketing context means 'bowling an unexpectedly fast ball'.

Pulling together

No matter how experienced or talented a rowing crew may be as individual rowers, their success in races depends largely on how well they row together. Experience has shown that crews who row in unison will often beat those with greater experience but who lack a unified rhythm. 'Pulling together' sums this up aptly.

The expression was widely adopted as rowing developed as a sport, although 'pulling together' and similar turns of phrase must have been used for hundreds of years whenever a group of people rowed together in a boat. In a general sense 'pulling together' means 'cooperating' and 'working together' to achieve a shared objective.

Pulling your punches

Boxers who 'pull their punches' deliberately lessen the force of their blows by pulling back their fists at the moment of impact, thereby sparing their opponents the full weight of their attack. 'Pulling punches' is widely used as a metaphor and those who 'pull their punches' in other situations 'hold back' to some extent and therefore spare the feelings of those at whom the 'punches' are addressed. The phrase is also applied in a negative sense, meaning that no attempt has been made to avoid giving offence or upsetting someone, as in the expression 'The manager didn't pull his punches in the dressing-room after the team lost what should have been an easy game.'

Pulling your weight

Here is another rowing term, this time directed at a member of the crew who does not put all his or her effort into each stroke. 'Pulling your weight' means putting all the strength in your body into moving the boat along. Anyone not 'pulling their weight' is a drag on the rest of the crew and something of a passenger. The phrase is used in many group activities, both team sports and other collective undertakings, to mean putting in maximum effort.

Punch-drunk

One of the hazards of boxing is damage caused to the brain over a period of time by persistent blows to the head. This can lead to a form of concussion which results in an unsteady gait reminiscent of the staggering progress made by those who have had too much to drink. In its figurative usage, 'punch-drunk' retains this sense of stupefaction; either from enduring heavy punishment when it is applied in situations such as 'He left the court punch-drunk by the sentence handed down by the magistrate', or from a feeling of euphoria as in 'He was punch-drunk with his success'.

Put through your paces

Horses are trained to move at a set series of 'paces': walk, trot, canter and gallop. In order to assess their capabilities and the quality of their training, prospective buyers like to see them 'put through their paces', to judge how they perform. The same expression is applied to individuals or organizations undergoing assessment and evaluation. If someone refers to being 'put through their paces' they mean that they are being watched closely while they undergo tests to see how they perform under all circumstances.

Regatta

The first 'regattas' were held on the Grand Canal in Venice during the seventeenth century, since when the word has been applied to competitions for all types of water craft. 'Regatta' is derived from the Venetian Italian word *rigatta* which meant 'a strife' or 'contention' and a 'struggle for supremacy'. This had close connections with trade as the Italian verb *rigattare* ('to wrangle' and 'sell by retail') shows. As the power and wealth of Venice was built on water-borne trade, it seems appropriate that races between boats should allude to this.

Rest on your oars

Rowing flat out in a rowing race is exhausting even for very fit rowers. Lifting the equivalent of a sack of potatoes from your ankles to your chest up to thirty-seven times a minute for six minutes leaves you breathless and limp at the finish. That is why rowers 'rest on their oars' while they recover and the term has been borrowed by other strenuous activities in the sense of 'taking a breathing space'.

Right off the bat

Baseball has supplied this 'punchy' turn of phrase which means 'right away'. The allusion is to a batter who strikes the first ball pitched at him or her cleanly and with sufficient power to send it flying far into the outfield, enabling the batter to set off straightaway to make a run.

Ringside seat

The most popular seats at a boxing match are those beside the ring, which offer a close and uninterrupted view of the fight. These are referred to as 'ringside seats' and their favoured location has led to the term being applied to other situations in which 'spectators' are afforded a privileged view of proceedings. These are not always organized events. 'Ringside seats' can refer to events which happen unexpectedly, as might be the case in an expression like 'We had ringside seats when the balloon landed right next to us'.

Riposte

'Riposte' is a term from fencing which is applied to an offensive movement made after an attack has been parried. This usually amounts to a 'return thrust' and here the origin of 'riposte' is evident. In French, a *riposte* is a 'retort' and a 'smart reply', which aptly describes the fencing movement. English has taken both senses and uses 'riposte' to mean a 'forceful reply' as well as a 'counterstroke'.

Roaring game

The 'roaring game' is a nickname for curling. This winter game played on frozen ponds, lakes and ice-rinks, achieved great popularity in Scotland where the nickname evolved. The 'roaring' in curling apparently comes from two sources. Curling stones are said to make to make a 'roaring' noise as they travel across the ice and in Scotland spectators and players both show their support for their teams with loud and enthusiastic cheering.

Rope in your pocket

This strange expression came into being as a result of an equally curious superstition. In days gone by it was believed that carrying in your pocket a piece of rope with which a man had been hanged would bring you success at cards. As a consequence of this, 'having a rope in your pocket' became an expression applied to people who were habitually lucky at cards.

Rub of the green

The 'rub of the green' is a golfing term used when a ball in motion is stopped or deflected by something. When this happens, the outcome can either favour or disadvantage the golfer who struck the ball. The ball could be deflected onto the green, for example, thereby improving the golfer's chances of hitting it into the hole. On the other hand, it could just as easily be deflected away from the green, into a bunker or some other obstacle. This element of chance has been taken into general usage, where the 'rub of the green' means a stroke of fortune which can be either good or ill depending on the outcome.

Running with the hare and hunting with the hounds

The hunting allusion in this time-honoured expression is to someone who is able to run with the quarry pursued by the hunt, while at the same time being with the hounds chasing that quarry. The meaning is clearly that anyone 'running with the hare and hunting with the hounds' is trying to keep in with two sides who are opposed to each other. 'Playing a double game' has a similar meaning.

Saved by the bell

The end of each round in a boxing match is signalled by the sound of a bell. If the bell rings while the referee is still counting out the ten seconds allowed to a knocked-down boxer to regain his feet, that boxer is said to have been 'saved by the bell'. However, the rules of boxing only allow a boxer to be saved from a knock-out verdict in professional boxing if the bell sounds at the end of the contest; at the end of any other round, the count continues. In amateur boxing the count continues after the bell which ends either the first or second round.

Say it ain't so, Joe!

This phrase expressing disbelief when an idol falls from grace, entered the language in the 1920s following accusations that the 1919 baseball World Series had been corrupted by bribery. Among those accused of deliberately losing the series at the behest of gamblers was 'Shoeless Joe' Jackson, a star of the Chicago White Sox team. He was called to give evidence before a grand jury looking into the allegations. As he left, a journalist reported a small boy asking him, 'It ain't so, Joe, is it?' to which Jackson apparently replied, 'Yes, kid, I'm afraid it is.' In retelling over the years, the boy's words were rearranged, but they lost nothing of his sense of disillusionment and betrayal.

Scooping the pool

'Scooping the pool' means winning all the money staked in a gambling game and by analogy to be 'totally successful' in any other venture. 'Pool' has an interesting history when used in this and similar expressions. Although spelt differently, it is derived from the French *poule*, meaning a 'hen'. This may be because hens were once set as the target or prize in games, as in the old *jeu de la poule* ('game of the hen').

Scoring an own goal

If a football player accidentally kicks the ball into his or her own goal, he or she is said to have 'scored an own goal', because the goal is awarded to the opposing team. The usage of 'scoring an own goal' has widened beyond the game of football to include anything which inadvertently benefits one's opponents, or which has a detrimental effect on oneself. It might be used in a statement like, 'Appointing someone who was much better qualified than him was an own goal as far his promotion prospects were concerned.'

Scratch race

Unlike the majority of races in which competitors are segregated according to age, weight and previous winnings, a 'scratch race' accepts any entrants, without imposing restrictions, and all of whom 'start from scratch' (below).

Selling a dummy

This is an expression much used in rugby. A 'dummy' is a feigned pass, designed to deceive opposing players. The player making the 'dummy' moves as if to pass the ball to a fellow player in the hope that tacklers on the other side will make for that player, therefore creating a gap in their defence through which the 'dummying' player can run. If the subterfuge is successful, the player who instigated it is said to have 'sold a dummy' to the opposing team.

Set the ball rolling

The first move in any ball game is to 'set the ball rolling'. This is a phrase which is used as a euphemism for the start of many activities, such as conversations and debates a well as other, non-ball, games.

Sharp set

Hawks which were hungry were described as being 'sharp set'
and from them the expression has broadened to refer to being
'hungry' in general.

Show the white feather

This expression which symbolizes cowardice dates from the time
when cockfighting was a popular national pastime. Since no
pure-bred gamecock had any white feathers in its plumage, a
bird with even a single white feather showed itself up as being of
inferior stock and therefore unlikely to show the fighting

characteristics of a thoroughbred. White feathers became a token of cowardice and during the First World War, men of fighting age who were seen wearing civilian clothes were liable to be handed white feathers by women who thought that they should be in uniform fighting for their country. The inference behind this was presumably that men who were not members of the armed forces must have been cowards.

Showing your hand

'Showing your hand' means disclosing your motives or intentions. It's an expression that derives from card games, in which players hide their cards until the game reaches the stage when they either choose, or are obliged, to reveal them.

Sick as a parrot

To feel as 'sick as a parrot' is the complete opposite to being 'over the moon'. Both rapidly became clichés in the 1970s and 1980s, firstly through their association with football players, managers and supporters and then after they were increasingly pilloried in the media. As an expression of huge disappointment and deflation following a let-down or failure, 'sick as a parrot' may have originated from a couple of possible sources. Parrots are well known to be susceptible to a range of ailments, notably the viral disease psittacosis (parrot fever). A 'dead parrot' was also the focus of one of the most popular sketches in the highly successful and influential comedy series *Monty Python's Flying Circus*, which was much in vogue in the early 1970s. 'Sick as a parrot' reflects both of these in the play on words which links 'sick' with 'diseased' and 'disgusted'.

Sin-bin

'Sin-bins', which originated in ice-hockey, have now become a feature of rugby. In both cases the 'sin-bin' is an area off the field of play in which players who have committed fouls are sent until the time penalty given to them has elapsed. The term has been taken up in slang to describe special units created in schools to house disruptive or otherwise difficult pupils while they receive special teaching aimed at reintegrating them into the main school environment.

Sitting on the splice

This is a colloquial expression, used in cricket and general conversation, in the sense of 'obstructing', similar to the meaning of 'stonewalling' (below). The 'splice' referred to is the narrow, V-shaped part of the cricket bat handle that is inserted into the top of the blade. Players intending to score runs aim to hit the ball with the lower part of the bat; striking with the splice provides very little 'leverage' and therefore puts little power into shot. The allusion here is to players who adopt a stubbornly defensive style of play, blocking deliveries with the bat, to prevent the ball hitting the stumps, but also greatly reducing their opportunities to score runs.

Skirting round

In the hunting field, a hound which cuts corners rather than following the true line of the scent left by a fox is known as a 'skirt'. Although the word is reserved almost exclusively these days for the familiar article of women's clothing, by the fifteenth century 'skirt' had acquired an additional meaning as a 'border' or 'edge', which is retained in 'skirting-board'. In the early nineteenth century 'skirter' was applied to a hunter who went round an obstacle rather than over or through it. Both these hunting references contribute to the present-day meaning of 'skirting round' which is used in the sense of 'avoiding' the main point of an issue by focusing on periphery elements.

Skittle out

Two games contribute to the origin of this phrase meaning 'swiftly to dispose of' people, or players in a game. 'Skittle out' became a term in cricket for getting out the batting side easily and quickly. It draws on a figurative reference to the game of 'skittles' (below), in which the stumps forming the wicket are knocked over with the same ease and rapidity as 'pins' are sent flying in 'skittles'.

Skittles

'Skittles' has been recorded in English as an alternative name for the game of ninepins since the seventeenth century. The origin of the word is uncertain, but the parallel name 'kittle pins' suggests a connection with a northern dialect word 'kittle' meaning 'to tickle'. If the origin of 'skittles' lies here, the allusion may be to 'touching' or 'tickling' the pins to make them fall down.

Snooker

The game of snooker, which embodies elements of billiards, pyramids and pool, developed among officers of the British army in India during the 1870s. The origins of the name are vague, but one military connection associates it with the slang term for first-year cadets at the Royal Military Academy, Woolwich. They were called 'snookers' by their superiors and by association 'snooker' developed as an expression of disdain. In the game, players who succeeded in leaving the cue ball in virtually unplayable positions were called 'snookers'. Since 'snookering' opponents became one of its principal tactics, it gave the game the name by which it is known today.

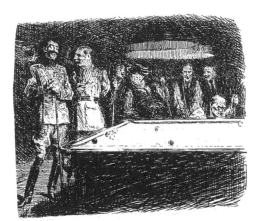

Southpaw

'Southpaw' has two meanings in two different sports: boxing and baseball. A fighter who boxes with the undorthodox stance of leading with his right hand and right leg is known as a 'southpaw'; the conventional stance leads with the left fist and left leg. In baseball, on the other hand, 'southpaw' is a nickname for a left-handed player, especially a pitcher; from this it has also come to be used occasionally for a left-handed person in general.

Spin doctor

'Spin doctor' is a political buzzword coined in the mid-1980s and now a standard feature of the political vocabulary of the English-speaking world. The phrase originated in America where 'spin' amounts to 'interpretation', or 'bias', put on information when it is made public and presented to the media. The allusion is to baseball, where 'spin' is one of the techniques used by a pitcher. 'Doctor' draws on various uses of the verb 'to doctor', in the sense of 'falsify' and 'alter'. And the role of the 'spin doctor' uses both these attributes to present events and policies to the media in a way which casts the most favourable light on the political party, or interest group, he or she represents.

Stalking-horse

This is another expression that has become part of the political vocabulary in the last twenty years. The original 'stalking-horses' were devices used by hunters to enable them to approach within range of game without scaring away their quarry. In practical terms a 'stalking-horse' was a hide-cum-decoy;

seemingly game sees no danger in a four-legged creature. The political usage of 'stalking-horse' dates from the mid-nineteenth century, when it began to be applied in American political circles to a candidate who was put forward to test the water for another candidate. In British politics a 'stalking-horse' has been used to challenge for the leadership of a political party. In this instance the 'stalking-horse' has been an MP with no realistic chance of being elected to the post. His role has been to gauge the weight of support for a challenge to the current leader and to reveal how well stronger candidates might fare in a leadership contest.

Starting from scratch

In the past it was customary for running races to start from a line scratched along the ground, hence the meaning of 'coming up to scratch' (above). Competitors who 'started from scratch' started at that line; those with a handicap were allowed to start ahead of it. This distinction gave rise to the figurative meaning of 'starting from scratch' which is 'to start from the very beginning', with no advantage.

Stone ginger

A 'stone ginger' is a 'certainty'. In racing terms it is a 'sure bet' and this is how the expression came into being. In the years immediately before the First World War, Stone Ginger was the name of a New Zealand racehorse which won every race it entered.

Stonewalling

This is a cricketing term for a player who bats simply to prolong play by blocking every ball and making no attempt to score runs. Such defensive measures do not make for an exciting game, but they can be instrumental in forcing a draw and so avoiding defeat. From this, 'stonewalling' has acquired the general meaning of adopting delaying or obstructive tactics.

Straight from the shoulder

'Straight from the shoulder' is a phrase from the boxing ring where it is applied to an orthodox punch, delivered by the leading glove, in a straight blow directly from the shoulder, as opposed to an upper-cut which comes from below. Punches 'straight from the shoulder' are used to wear down an opponent. In its figurative sense, 'straight from the shoulder' means 'direct' and 'frank', as in an expression like 'He gave me the bad news straight from the shoulder'.

Strike zone

In baseball, the 'strike zone' is the area in the batter's box, over the home plate between the batter's armpits and knees. Balls pitched inside the strike zone are valid pitches; those outside the strike zone are invalid. The 'strike zone' effectively represents the pitcher's target and this is the sense in which the phrase has been used in other contexts, notably precision air-attacks by guided bombs and missiles. Those on target are colloquially referred to as being 'in the strike zone'.

Striking the ball under the line

Before nets were introduced into tennis courts a line was strung across the playing area, above which players had to hit the ball. Any balls passing below the line were out of play. From tennis 'striking the ball under the line' transferred into general use where, by the middle of the sixteenth century, it had acquired the broad meaning of 'failing' in one's objective.

Stumped

In addition to being bowled and caught, players batting in games of cricket can be dismissed by being stumped. This requires agility and quick thinking on the part of the wicket-keeper, stationed behind the wicket. If the player batting misses the ball and is beyond (with both body and bat) the crease where he or she stands to face the bowling, the wicket-keeper can break the wicket with the ball and claim a 'stumping'. In its wider usage, 'stumped' retains a similar meaning of 'being outwitted', 'defeated' and 'at a loss'.

Stymie

'Stymie' originated as a golfing term, although it has been obsolete in golf for half a century. A 'stymie' occurred on a putting-green where a player was 'laid a stymie' if another player's ball fell in his or her line of putt to the hole. Only a difficult lofting shot could succeed in holing a ball in this situation. Such a predicament gave rise to several expressions that are still in use. As a noun, 'a stymie' is a 'frustrating predicament'. Used as a verb, 'to stymie' means to place someone in an awkward and discouraging position and 'to be stymied' means to be placed in such a situation.

Sucker punch

In boxing slang, a 'sucker punch' is an unorthodox punch which lands only through a surprise lapse on the part of the receiver. The phrase is used widely in other sports when an opponent, or an opposing side, make a 'soft' score by winning an easy point, scoring an easy goal, or touching down an easy try. In every case, describing such a setback as a 'sucker punch' implies an error, or lack of concentration, on the party of the other player, or the defending side.

Sweeping the board

In betting games in which all the stakes are placed on the table, a player who wins all the money staked is said to 'sweep the board'. The phrase is applied to other circumstances in which one contestant carries off all, or the majority, of the awards. Films that win more Academy Awards than any other entered in that year's competition are often described as having 'swept the board at the Oscars'.

Sweepstake

In the fifteenth century, a 'sweepstake' was a person who took the whole of the stakes in a game. By the eighteenth century it had acquired the meaning by which it is known today. A 'sweepstake' is a race or contest in which all the competitors pay a stake, which added together, provide the prize money awarded to the winner. 'Sweepstake' is also applied to a gambling arrangement, usually on a horse race, in which the sum of the participators' stakes goes to the drawer (or drawers) of winning (or placed) horses.

Taking a rain check

'Rain checks' entered general usage by way of sporting events in America. These were usually baseball games, in which a 'rain check' was a ticket which permitted the holder to be re-admitted to the game after it had had to be postponed because of rain. In the last fifty years the term has broadened to mean a 'deferment'. 'Let's take a rain check on that' means 'let's put that on hold for the time being'. It is also used as an acceptance of an invitation for a later date, as in 'I'll take a rain check on that', meaning 'I'm sorry I can't come on this occasion, but please invite me next time.'

Taking the ball before the bound

This is a metaphor from cricket which alludes to a player who is over hasty with the bat and who tries to strike the ball prematurely. Applied figuratively, it means 'anticipating an opportunity'.

Taking the strain

'Strain' has been used since the thirteenth century to mean to 'draw tight' and 'to stretch'. In a tug of war, 'Take the strain' is the command given to teams to prepare them to pull on the rope, in other words to get ready for the contest proper. As a metaphor, 'taking the strain' means getting ready for a major exertion, either physical or mental.

Taking up the running

This expression is applied in both athletics and horse racing to a runner who moves forward from the field during the course of a race, to assume the lead. In doing this, the horse or athlete sets the pace that the rest of the competitors must follow if they are to stay in contention. In its metaphorical sense, 'taking up the running' means 'taking over the leading role' in an organization or enterprise.

Taking your eye off the ball

'Taking your eye off the ball' has become a well-worked turn of phrase in politics. The allusion is to a player in any ball game who momentarily allows his or her attention to be deflected from the ball, resulting in a mishit, or a missed kick. In politics, the expression is applied to politicians who 'lose sight' of the main thrust of policy, or who fail to pick up public reaction to an issue or initiative. In either case they are said to have 'lost sight of the ball' when public opinion or a reaction to a policy turns against them.

That rings a bell

'That rings a bell' is another way of saying 'That sounds familiar', or 'That looks familiar'. The expression may have originated from the fairground competition in which contestants tried their strength by wielding a large mallet. The object of this test was to hit a pivot at the base of a tall column, which sent a projectile shooting upwards. If the bell at the top of the column was struck, it rang confirming that whoever struck the blow was particularly strong.

The bigger they come, the harder they fall

In its present use 'the bigger they come the harder they fall' is a proverb attributed to the boxer Bob Fitzsimmons. In the 1890s and early 1900s Fitzsimmons won world titles boxing at three weights: middleweight, light-heavyweight and heavyweight. Never weighing more than 167 pounds (76 kilograms) he defeated a succession of much bigger men and once took only two rounds to beat an opponent to whom he was conceding 140 pounds (64 kilograms). Since his time the phrase has been taken up as a statement of defiance in all walks of life. However, earlier references to this, or very similar turns of phrase date back to the end of the fifteenth century.

The Devil's bedpost

This is the nickname in card games for the four of clubs. It leads to a similar nickname, the 'Devil's four-poster', which is a hand of cards containing four clubs. Among whist players it was once said that there was a never a good hand which contained four clubs.

The game isn't over till it's over

'Yogi' Berra, the American baseball player and coach is attributed with coining this phrase during the 1973 season when his team, the New York Mets, were in contention for the National League pennant. Berra told reporters, and laid down a warning to rival teams, that the Mets would keep up the challenge right until the final minute of the final game. His words have been echoed in an equally forceful manner by sports managers, politicians and military leaders.

The game's afoot

'The game's afoot' is a term from hare coursing; the 'game' here being the hare itself. Having broken cover and started a run for safety, the hare would have been spotted by the hounds, which would have set off in pursuit. This sense is carried into the figurative use of the expression, in which 'the game's afoot' would have been used to mean that something 'has started'. Shakespeare puts it stirringly into the mouth of Henry V at the siege of Harfleur, at the end of one of the few scenes in English drama which is occupied solely by a speech given by one character,

And you, good yeomen,
Whose limbs were made in England, show us here
The mettle of your pasture; let us swear
That you are worth your breeding – which I doubt not;
For there is none of you so mean and base
That hath not noble lustre in your eyes,
I see you stand like greyhounds in the slips,
Straining upon the start. The game's afoot:
Follow your spirit; and upon this charge
Cry 'God for Harry, England, and Saint George!'

The game's not worth the candle

The allusion here is to gambling at cards by candlelight. In this
expression the game has reached the point where there is so
little money to be won that it does not even amount to the price
of a fresh candle that would enable it to be continued.
Therefore anything described as not being 'worth the candle' is
not worth either the trouble or expense involved in doing it.

The gloves are off

Until the adoption of the Queensberry Rules, which regulated boxing in the second half of the nineteenth century, prize-fighting comprised bare-fist boxing matches that sometimes lasted for two hours or longer. These were brutal contests in which the combatants suffered terrible beatings. The Queensberry Rules introduced the wearing of boxing gloves. So, references to fighting without gloves implied a cruder, harsher contest in which no mercy was shown by either side. These days 'the gloves are off' means that, whatever the competition is, it will be conducted in earnest with little quarter given.

The Noble Science

This is a euphemism used for both boxing and fencing, both of which amount to 'the noble art of self-defence'.

The real McCoy

The sporting origin of this expression appears to rest with the American welterweight boxer 'Kid' McCoy, who was at the height of his fame in the 1890s. According to the oft-told anecdote, McCoy was challenged by a drunk in a bar, who refused to believe his friends when they warned him who he was provoking. McCoy apparently did his best to avoid retaliating, but finally had little option but to hit the man, knocking him out in the process. When he came round, the drunk admitted ruefully, 'You're right, it's the real McCoy.' Since then the phrase has been used as an expression of irrefutable authenticity, in the sense of 'the genuine article'.

The whole shoot

Anyone who goes 'the whole shoot' does all there is to do to achieve a particular end. In this sense, you could use other metaphors such as 'going the whole hog'. The allusion in 'the whole shoot' is to the hunting field in which the 'whole shoot' is a sustained volley of shots in which everything is fired at the game which have been put up, leaving nothing in reserve.

Three strikes and you're out

'Three strikes and you're out' (often abbreviated to 'three strikes') became a byword for American right-wing politicians and their followers in the 1980s and early 1990s for taking a firm hand with law enforcement. 'Three-strikes' legislation was passed in a number of US states, by which offenders convicted of three serious felonies received a mandatory sentence of life imprisonment. The 'three-strikes' reference is to baseball, in which a batter who has had three strikes (three valid pitches) and has failed to hit the ball, is out.

Throw in your hand

'Throwing in your hand' means to stop playing in a card game; your 'hand' being the cards you are holding. Used as a metaphor, it means giving up something on the basis that it is hopeless to continue with it.

Throwing in the sponge

If, during the course of a boxing match, a sponge (used to refresh a boxer) was tossed into a ring by one of the contestant's ringside team, it was a sign that the man was beaten and the fight over; 'throwing in the towel' has the same meaning. In its wider usage the phrase implies that whoever is 'throwing in the sponge' is giving up and admitting defeat.

Throwing your hat into the ring

This has the opposite meaning to 'throwing in the sponge'. By 'throwing your hat into the ring' you are laying down, or accepting a challenge. The metaphor is drawn from prizefighting at fairs and similar ad-hoc competitions, at which boxers offered to take on all comers, and bets were placed on the outcome of these rough-and-ready contests.

Time out

'Time out' is one of several terms derived from American sports that have found their way into general English usage. In American games, such as baseball, 'time out' refers to a brief intermission in play, from which has evolved its broader meaning of a 'short break' in work or other any other activity; as in 'I'm taking time out from writing this report'.

Toeing the line

At the start of a race all competitors must have their feet just behind the starting line, which means with their toes just touching the line. From this, 'toeing the line' has come to be used as a metaphor meaning 'conforming' and 'accepting discipline' imposed by others.

Top hole!

As a phrase that was at the height of its popularity a century ago, 'top hole!' means 'excellent' and 'the very best'. It probably owes its origin to the holes or notches cut into a board to record points scored in a game. The holes at the top of the board represent the highest score and therefore the best score.

Toss up

A 'toss up' is an even chance; a state of affairs which could result in one of two ways. It is used in expressions like 'Because of the weather, it's a toss up if the picnic will happen'. The phrase comes from the tossing of a coin, which is used to determine the start of various games. Participants call 'heads' or 'tails' and the outcome is agreed by whichever side of the coin lands face up.

Touché

'Touché' is a French word meaning 'touched' or 'hit'. It is the term used in fencing to acknowledge a hit. By extension it is also used to acknowledge a telling remark, or riposte, made by an opponent in an argument.

Trumps

The origin of the word 'trump', when used in card games, is the French *triomphe*, meaning a 'triumph'. 'Trump' has been used in English since the sixteenth century to mean a card of a suit that ranks above all others. Colloquially, 'trumps' is used in expressions like 'coming up trumps', meaning 'proving to be useful at an opportune moment'.

Turn the tables

In its figurative usage, 'turning the tables' on someone means to 'reverse' the conditions or relationship between you and them. This might occur in a legal action in which one party 'turns the tables' on someone suing them, by launching a counter-suit. The allusion here is to reversing the 'table', or board, in games such as chess or draughts, with the result that an opponent's position is altered to their disadvantage.

Turn-up for the book

A 'turn-up for the book' is a stroke of unexpected good fortune; which phrase derives from horse racing, where the book referred to is the record of bets laid. When a 'turn-up for the book' occurs, it usually means that a horse with long odds, that is one not expected to win, does in fact win, netting a substantial pay-out for those backing it.

Twelfth man

In a cricket team, the 'twelfth man' is a reserve player, who is only called on as a substitute when one of the selected eleven has to leave the field. By extension, 'twelfth man' is used in other contexts with reference to anyone who just misses attaining distinction.

Two strings to your bow

Whether in warfare or hunting, wise bowmen always carried spare bow-strings in case the ones fitted to their bows broke. The same implicit precaution and forward-thinking applies when the phrase is used as a metaphor. 'Having two strings to your bow' in its wider usage means to have 'two ways of achieving an objective'.

Under starter's orders

This is the instruction given by the official starter of a horse-race, telling jockeys to line up, so that the order to start racing can be given. Once a race is 'under starter's orders' all bets placed on it are operative and no more can be laid. To be 'under starter's orders' in any situation means to be 'ready to race', 'awaiting the signal to begin'.

Upping the ante

In poker, the 'ante' is the stake put up by a player before drawing new cards. 'Ante' has been used in this context since the nineteenth century, although it is a direct borrowing from Latin, in which *ante* means 'before' or 'in front'. Thus 'upping the ante' means increasing the stakes, literally or metaphorically.

Upset the apple-cart

To 'upset the apple-cart' is a colloquial term in wrestling when one wrestler throws an opponent. The phrase, or ones very like it, date back to ancient times and today to 'upset the apple-cart' means to 'disrupt plans or arrangements'.

We wuz robbed!

As a cry of anguish and distress after a defeat (usually a sporting one) 'We wuz robbed!' was coined by the American boxing manager, Joe Jacobs. In 1932, Max Schmeling, a heavyweight boxer represented by Jacobs, lost in a title fight against Jack Sharkey. Jacobs was incensed at the result and, convinced that his camp had been cheated, he protested into the microphone 'We wuz robbed!' His words have become a sporting cliché on a par with later ones, notably 'over the moon' and 'sick as a parrot'.

Weighing in

The 'weigh-in' forms an important part of the build-up to a boxing match. This is the event when the two boxers appear in 'fighting form' in public for the first time, allowing commentators and the media to assess their physical condition. The 'weigh-in' also serves the practical purpose of confirming the respective weights of the contenders, which may have some bearing on the outcome of the fight. 'Weigh-ins' occur in horse racing as well. Here the 'weight' carried by a horse comprises the weight of the jockey and everything else carried by the horse except whip, bridle, plates and anything worn on the horse's legs. The phrase also has a colloquial usage meaning 'to intervene' with something, as a statement like 'He weighed in with a question about funding policy'.

Weight for age race

This is a type of handicap in which horses carry different weights according to a set of agreed criteria. All things being equal, horses of the same age carry the same weight.

When the chips are down

The allusion here is to the point in a game of poker when all the bets have been placed, but the outcome is still uncertain. As a metaphor, such a situation takes on a dramatic air in which 'when the chips are down' means when things come to the point of action.

Whistle blower

'Whistle blower' is the term applied to informers, who make public, or otherwise expose, malpractice and corruption. Although not directly instrumental in punishing offenders, 'whistle blowers' draw attention to what is going on. The allusion is to the referee in a football match, who blows a whistle to stop play when a foul is committed. 'Whistle blowers' are often employees in corporations, or civil servants, who risk their own jobs and career opportunities in exposing the misconduct of others.

Whole new ball game

A 'whole new ball game' is something that is 'totally different'. Although superficially the circumstances may be familiar, as is the case with a game like baseball, from which the expression derives, the use of a 'whole new ball game' emphasizes the fact that something completely new is in the offing.

Wild-goose chase

In the Middle Ages a 'wild-goose chase' was a game played on horseback in which riders had to follow a course which veered and changed direction erratically, much as a wild-goose does in flight. From this, a 'wild-goose chase' has become a metaphor for an impractical or hopeless undertaking.

Win at a canter

A 'canter' is an easy gallop and an abbreviation for the 'Canterbury pace', which was the comfortable pace at which mounted pilgrims were thought to have ridden to Canterbury. Therefore a horse which 'wins at a canter' has an easy victory over its competitors. In such a situation the horse is so far in front of the rest of the field that the jockey can afford to ease its pace to a gentle run to the finish. The expression is applied to other 'wins' on and off the sporting field and all carry the same sense of winning with considerable ease.

Winning by a short head

This is a much closer margin of victory than 'winning at a canter'. In horse racing terminology, a 'head' is one of the official measurements used to estimate distances between horses as they pass the winning-post. A 'head' is clearly the length of a horse's head, and a short head measures less than that. So 'winning [anything] by short head' means winning by a very narrow margin.

Winning hands down

Horse racing also supplies this metaphor for an easy victory. In most races, jockeys need to keep careful hold on the reins to be sure of getting the best performance from their mounts. However, in a race where one horse is so far in front that it cannot be caught, its jockey can afford to relax his or her hold on the reins, while still being confident of 'winning hands down'. The analogy is used in many other situations where victory and success are secured with little effort.

Winning isn't everything, it's the only thing

This catchphrase, coined in American football during the 1950s and 1960s, brushes aside the gentlemanly approach to sporting contests and introduces a grainier attitude to success and failure that came to characterize both professional and amateur sport in the second half of the twentieth century. Vince Lombardi, coach and manager of the Green Bay Packers football team is credited with first coining the phrase (or something very like it). Others followed him and in due course the sentiment was taken up as a political campaigning slogan. In the 1972 US presidential contest 'Winning in politics isn't everything, it's the only thing' was the catchphrase of Richard Nixon's supporters.

Winning the wooden spoon

This is a euphemism for 'coming last', the wooden spoon being a booby prize awarded to competitors who trail in behind the rest of the field. Although it is well known in a sporting context, the expression was actually coined in an academic context: a wooden spoon being awarded to the student who came last in the final mathematical exams at Cambridge University.

Win one for the Gipper

This became a catchphrase popularized by Ronald Reagan during his political career. As the explanation shows, it was used to characterize an act of selfless triumph in the face of apparently insurmountable odds, inspired by a noble sentiment. Reagan acquired the expression from a character he played in a 1940 film about American football. Reagan's character, George Gipp, was a real-life football star who had died of pneumonia in December 1920 at the age of twenty-five. On his deathbed he told Knute Rockne, the coach of the Notre Dame team for which Gipp had played, 'Some time, Rock, when the team's up against it, when things are wrong and the breaks are beating the boys – tell them to go in there with all they've got and win just one for the Gipper.' Eight years after George Gipp died, Notre Dame were having a terrible season. Having lost to the Army 18–0 in the previous year's game, they were in New York to face them again. In the locker room, Rockne repeated Gipp's

deathbed request. 'I've never used Gipp's request until now,' he told them. 'This is that game. It's up to you.' His team went out and played like men possessed, beating the Army 12-6. The following day the *New York Daily News* carried the headline 'Gipp's Ghost beats Army'. From then on the game was known as 'the Gipp Game'. With this inspiring tale to recall a fine moment in recent American history, Ronald Reagan was not shy about urging his supporters and later his countrymen to 'Win one for the Gipper'.

Yarborough

This is the name given to a hand at bridge in which there are no trumps. It was originally applied to a hand with no card higher than a nine. The name comes from the second Lord Yarborough who used regularly to bet up to 1000:1 against any such hand appearing in a game in which he took part.

You can run, but you can't hide

In the world heavyweight boxing championship fight in the summer of 1946 Joe Louis was lined up against Billy Cotten. Cotten was known to be a fast mover, but Louis was unimpressed and warned, 'He can run, but he can't hide.' When they met in the ring, Joe Louis's words proved to be true and he won the title with a knockout. The phrase passed into popular usage and in 1985, following a terrorist hijack of an American airliner in Beirut, President Reagan warned those responsible that they would be hunted down and caught, rephrasing Joe Louis's words as 'You can run, but you can't hide.'

You cannot be serious

This exclamation of incredulity and fury became popular in the 1980s in emulation of similar outbursts by the American tennis champion John McEnroe against match officials. Umpires and linesmen at tennis championships around the world, who called decisions with which McEnroe disagreed, were frequently subjected to tirades which earned McEnroe the nickname 'Superbrat'.